Freemasonry
as a Way of Awakening

By Rémi Boyer

The Ways of Awakening Trilogy

Freemasonry as a Way of Awakening

*Mask Cloak Silence:
Martinism as a Way of Awakening*

*Beneath the Veil of Elias Artista
The Rose-Croix as a Way of Awakening:
An Oral Tradition*
(with Lima de Freitas and Manuel Gandra)

*The Rectified Scottish Rite:
From the Doctrine of Reintegration
to the* Imago Templi

With Sylvie Boyer-Camax

*Letters to Friends of the Spirit:
Martinist Views & Others*

The Way Without Masters

Freemasonry as a Way of Awakening

AN ESSAY FOR PRAGMATIC MASONIC
AND POST-MASONIC INITIATION

Rémi Boyer

Rose Circle Publications
Bayonne NJ
2020

Freemasonry as a Way of Awakening

Copyright © 2020 by Rémi Boyer
English translation copyright © 2020 by Michael Sanborn

Thanks to Howard Doe for his invaluable suggested improvements to the translation draft.

ISBN: 978-1-947907-10-2
Library of Congress Control Number: 2020915245

First published in French as *La Franc-maçonnerie comme voie d'eveil* by Éditions Rafael de Surtis, 2006. Second edition published under the title *La Franc-maçonnerie, une spiritualité vivante* by Éditions Le Mercure Dauphinois, 2010.

Cover painting: *O pórtico* by Lima de Freitas, acrylic on canvas, 1992.
Courtesy of Helle Hartvig de Freitas.

Special thanks to Genevieve Dubois, director of Éditions Le Mercure Dauphinois, for support of this U.S. edition.

Book design and layout by Michael Sanborn, TextArc LLC. michael@textarc.net

All rights reserved. No part of this publication may be reproduced, distributed, or transmitted in any form or by any means, including photocopying, recording, or other electronic or mechanical methods, without the prior written permission of the publisher, except in the case of brief quotations embodied in critical reviews and certain other non-commercial uses permitted by copyright law. For permission requests, write to the publisher at the address below.

Rose Circle Publications
P.O. Box 854
Bayonne, NJ 07002, U.S.A.
www.rosecirclebooks.com

This essay is dedicated to all
the *free masons*
who knew how to escape forms
to recognize the liberatory essence
of the quest.

All my thanks go to the four Watchers:
Robert Amadou
Claude Bruley
Lima de Freitas
Jean-Louis Larroque

Contents

	Foreword	xi
	Preface	xv
	Preface to the First Edition	xix
	Preface to the Second Edition	xxiii
	Against gentrification	xxiii
	In the margins, the center	xxv
	Rites, what are they for?	xxviii
	Initiation itself	xxxi
	WARNING	1
1	OF INITIATION...	3
2	THE INITIATORY APPROACH	15
	1. The request for initiation	16
	2. Analysis of the initiation request	20
	3. The passage under the blindfold	22
	4. Initiation instruction and orientation to the tradition	24
	5. The "first" initiation	25
	6. The initiatory work	26
	7. The evaluation	27
3	THE INITIATORY WORK, PROJECT, AND SETTING	29
	The two great functions of initiatory work	29
	The initiatory project	30
	Nested settings	31

4	**SPACE, TIME, AND COMPANIONAGE**	35
	Space and time	35
	Rules and knowledge	38
	The Companionage	39
5	**THE INITIATORY PROCESS**	43
	The investment of initiatory work	43
	The three phases of the initiatory process	47
6	**ASSESSMENT OF THE INITIATORY PROCESS**	51
	The triangle: referent-initiator-Self	51
	Assessment and self-assessment	53
7	**THE THEORY OF "THREE PERSONS" IN THE INITIATORY PROCESS**	55
	The secular person and the sacred person	55
	The witness, third person	57
	The posture of the third person	58
	The culmination of the process	59
8	**DYSFUNCTIONS IN THE INITIATORY PROCESS**	61
	Dysfunctions in the group or obedience	61
	Dysfunctions in one or the other person	63
	Dysfunctions of the witness	67
9	Questions and Answers	69
	TRANSITIONAL CONCLUSION	89
	THREE INITIATORY VIGNETTES	93
	INTERVIEWING A CANDIDATE BENEATH THE BLINDFOLD	95
	WORKING PROPOSALS FOR A LODGE OF THE EGYPTIAN RITE	105
	Objectives for the first three degrees	105
	Development of each meeting	107

Apprentice of the Craft — 113
Form — 113
Theme: the alignment of the four bodies — 115

Companion of the Craft — 117
Form — 117
Theme: lighting the flaming star — 118

Master of the Craft — 123
Form — 123
Theme: the formation of the Body of Glory
   (lighting the seven-branched candlestick) — 124

How to Ascend to the Upper Chamber — 127
The Temple, representation of the human body — 127
From the upper chamber to the top of the head — 128
Operate after rising — 130
The holy mountain — 131
The upper chamber — 132
The middle chamber — 132
Cagliostro plays the architect — 133

How to Ascend to the Middle Chamber — 137
To operate effectively — 137
You have experienced this state — 137
A three-step process — 138
The consequences — 139

When Philosophers Related This Experience — 141

Foreword

Having been privileged to work with Rémi Boyer for many years, I hail this outstanding volume as the indispensable aid to anyone contemplating Masonic or any other initiation, as it clearly explains the nature of true initiation and spiritual progress.

It is not a comfortable book, as it makes clear that whilst an experienced and properly prepared initiator can guide the seeker on the early stages of his journey, the practices and efforts required are not easy and require a level of dedication which must be long-lasting and very clearly focused.

Rémi teaches the essential doctrine of the Awakening (*L'Éveil*) that is often expressed as listening in silence to the essential intervals between the notes. It involves the rigorous examination of the Self in order to eliminate negative attitudes and behavior, ceasing to be driven by popular trends or media, and being no longer what Martinists term "a man of the stream," like a cork bobbing along in a fast-flowing river without any sense of destination or direction.

He also explores the nature of consciousness so that one perceives oneself "through the perception of the divine game of energy and consciousness" and feels free to "elect" courses of action, through use of the awakened consciousness rather than mere instinct or imitation.

Freemasonry, as practiced today, is all too often driven by mundane notions of personal advancement through the hierarchy, traditional rituals learned by heart (but not really understood), charitable giving, and dining in the pleasant company of friends. It thereby becomes of purely historical and cultural interest rather than practicing and promoting true spiritual growth. It is like an overripe fruit in which, whilst the outer skin looks appealing, the essential fruit within has withered away.

Rémi speaks at length of the need to prepare the Candidate thoroughly, first by getting him to articulate clearly what he is seeking through the initiatic path, how he sees his present self, and at what point he feels he has arrived at in his present life. He must understand that he has to devote much personal time and effort to the Quest and endeavor to acquire and maintain a balanced frame of mind. This can be achieved by in-depth interviews and by encouraging the Candidate to present a paper, as is done in many European esoteric systems, about how he sees his way forward and why he seeks initiation.

The passage under the blindfold is very well described. It involves the recognition that the Candidate is on his own within himself, stepping into the unknown and away from the familiar, but at the same time relying on unknown brethren to help him to progress. The process of initiation is therefore a stripping away of the former exoteric self and substituting a rigorous reappraisal of one's whole being—a catharsis.

The so-called intervals between the notes or words of the ritual are the reaction of the inner self to align the Candidate with the doctrines of the group and to develop his own path of awakening. The initiate then starts to build his own inner temple.

In the Companionate or Fellowcraft degree, the Candidate needs to work to fit himself for his rebirth into his new life. That is why he needs to read and study the fruits of other avatars' experiences, as symbolized by the exhortation to studying the seven liberal arts and sciences, which study defines the true Renaissance Man. This is perhaps one of the worst trends of modern Freemasonry. In the original rituals the Candidate could expect informal and unscripted questions, the answers to which were meant to reveal whether he had really studied enough to prepare himself properly for the next important part of his journey towards becoming a Master Mason. Instead, Lodges today have even formalized the questions so that all the Candidate needs to do is to give parrot-like answers to a list of questions, the answers to which have already been provided, a practice of zero value!

The studies in the Companionate should also teach him to identify the true seekers within his Lodge circle. He must also start to learn from this how to cope with what many writers have described as "the dark night of the soul" and to see it as an essential part of the growth of the personality. It occurs as the old self is being deconstructed and the new "I" is starting to permeate the individual's overall psyche. He also learns to recognize certain symbols which are eternal and are used to convey meanings that go far beyond normal human powers of description.

It is this change which has been compared to sitting in an art gallery contemplating a painting and suddenly, as it were, stepping through the frame so that one becomes not only part of the artwork but of all that surrounds him—he is one with all creation. This is what may be truly described as the silence of the Middle Chamber, where for the first time the Seeker gets a glimpse, however fleeting, of the true reality which he will then ever after strive to evolve into the sacred self that is the true alchemy.

Rémi also clarifies the status of Master. It is where the external instruction from the Lodge finally comes to an end and the legend of Hiram is finally enacted and needs to be understood. The Candidate is symbolically raised as the Body of Glory and the difference and similarities between the myth of Osiris and the Hiramic legend become clearly apparent. He will learn for himself how to perform the internal alchemy required to attain this goal and the role of the four deaths which ultimately purify the spirit.

The book also uses and quotes the experience and writings of some of the great esoteric practitioners such as Martinez de Pasqually, Cornelius Agrippa, and Louis-Claude de Saint Martin and shows how these can be utilized to gain a deeper understanding of the important allegories contained in the Bible and in other sacred works.

Perhaps the greatest achievement of this masterly volume is to provide indispensable guidelines that can be used as reference points to inspire, encourage, and measure spiritual progress; to realize that personal development can only be achieved through continual self-examination and by passing one's esoteric knowledge to others to help them along the Path.

The Awakening is the key concept that is vital to a true understanding of esoteric work and that is why this step-by-step analysis of how to achieve spiritual progress is a unique contribution to self-improvement and advancement in the cynical and materialist period of history which we currently inhabit.

Howard Doe

Preface

by José M. Anes, passed Grand Master of
the Regular Grand Lodge of Portugal

RÉMI BOYER—WHO WITH ROBERT AMADOU founded and gave life to the very interesting magazine *L'Esprit des Choses* (in which I was able to participate as a member of the editorial board, alongside, among others, our friend Massimo Introvigne) and *La Lettre du Crocodile*, a useful bibliographic bulletin, is a very serious and competent researcher in the field of esotericism and initiatory ways.

He joins to a historical and doctrinal erudition, a thorough knowledge of certain ways. He has published several books in the field of the paths of awakening and the sacred erotic—*Le Fou de Shakti, Éveil et incohérisme, Érotique et érotisme, Quelques folles considérations sur l'Absolu*, etc.—which testify to a great knowledge, of a true wisdom based on great personal experience of the various initiatory horizons.

Rémi Boyer has animated and directed several initiatory groups and orders, explored several Western and Eastern ways, from Rhenish mysticism to the philosophies of awakening, including Gnosticism and Hermeticism.

I met Rémi Boyer and our mutual friend, Jean-Louis Larroque, on the paths of operational esotericism, paths that I began to go through before I was initiated into Freemasonry: alchemy, Rosicrucianism, the Portuguese mythical tradition, Templarism, Martinism, and others. What impressed me in his approach is the maintenance, in all dimensions of initiation, of a posture that leads from the complex to the simple, from the multiple to the one. This attitude, derived from a sense of presence, this availability to awakening, knows how to impress on his "life" all the ways in which he exercises his mastery, and he shares them to encourage us to pass, in his own words, from the gesture to the *Geste*.[1]

That is why we were awaiting the publication of his work on Freemasonry, a domain in which he has travelled through various Rites and Obediences.[2]

Here is a universe that is familiar to me. After having been initiated into the Grand Orient of Lusitania, I participated in the founding and development of the Regular Grand Lodge of Portugal[3] of which I was the third Grand Master. Independently of the discussions, in this case very respectable, which cross the various fields of the Masonic universe, it should be reaffirmed that in Freemasonry, whatever the Rite, whatever the obedience, awakening and presence is at the heart of the process that gives access to Initiation. And it is in this area that this book by Rémi Boyer[4] proves to be an indispensable tool for any Freemason who seeks Initiation.

---

[1] In French, *geste* can mean both "gesture" and "saga" or "heroic deeds."—Trans.

[2] To understand this complex world, I advise the reader to follow the excellent *Guide pratique de la Franc Marçonnerie—rites, systèmes, organisations,* 2nd ed., by Jean Solis (Paris: Dervy, 2004).

[3] Under the name Grande Loge Légale du Portugal/GLRP, after the 1996/97 schism—or, as our English friends like to say, the Grand Regular (Legal) Lodge of Portugal.

[4] In the tradition of other books like *La voie du Franc-maçon—techniques initiatiques de la Franc-maçonnerie* by Jules Mérias (Paris: Dervy, 2000).

Freemasonry has many dimensions, spiritual, philosophical, social, political (not in the sense of the politician), it encourages fraternity, mutual aid and conviviality, but it really asserts itself as an initiatory Order only by the individual effort and commitment of each Freemason to constitute and create a sacred space and time, not only in the Temple, but also in their own interiority. Only then is potential initiation actualized.

As a Freemason, always in search of the Light, I thank Rémi Boyer for this remarkable *Geste* of initiatory Charity that constitutes the writing of such a book!

J.M.A.
Caparica, Portugal
Spring Equinox of 2006

Preface to the First Edition

For a practice of Masonic and post-Masonic initiation

by Jean-Pierre Giudicelli de Cressac Bachelerie

AFTER PUBLISHING VARIOUS WORKS that refer to esoteric, literary and philosophical traditions, Rémi Boyer wrote this essay dedicated to "all freedmen." "Another book on Freemasonry!" some readers will think, and yet this one has a marked difference. It poses the problems of Masonic initiation and even defines its praxis. This book is also an inquiry that will provoke a debate, because there are two Masonic concepts that are very difficult to grasp.

For Rémi Boyer, the Masonic path is not only an apprenticeship of freedom in the widest sense of the term, but a way of awakening, even, in its more internal aspects, a theurgy. Always a poet, Rémi quotes the Comte de Lautréamont: "Sleep is a reward for some, a torment for others. For all, it is a sanction." Of course, that's what it's all about, getting out of the world of sleep and dreams, the "sanction," and without a doubt, getting out others with a similar quest. As a contemporary existentialist philosopher wrote: "How can I be free if others are not?"

The author also directly expressed the essence of the Masonic way: "The ceremonial can be replaced by a series of self-remembering exercises." Indeed, all of the Masonic way should be attention and presence in the moment. That is why the ritual is a permanent recall to the axis of the present: "It is midday... It is midnight." The work begins on the vertical until by force of his travels, the Apprentice, then Companion, finds himself finally Master in the Middle Chamber, where the self watches over him, after he has risen from the world of the dead. For years, the Mason learned by rote the signs of order and the various reminders included in the ritual, punctuated with knocks of the mallet of the Venerable Master who, in the East, is responsible for keeping the brothers awake.

In the Masonic ritual, as the author rightly emphasizes, everything should be a "self-reminder," which would prevent many Masons from making a muddle of things, dwelling on sociological or mercantile horizontality, depending on whether the seeker is in one obedience or another. The notion of obedience itself is subversive, because true Masonry is "a Free Mason in a Free Lodge." By 1863, Ragon had already written: "The number of Masonries exceeds sixty. It is easy to understand that these productions are Masonic only in form: they are all different [...] This mass of rites is only due to the speculative manufacture of high grades, from which there result as many schisms as rites. True Masonry, composed of three degrees, does not cause schisms."

Already interested in all aspects of esotericism, I had the advantage of being guided to Masonry by a teacher who had written an essay, "The Words of Brother Nemo." He lived in Monte Carlo. This mysterious person (Jo. C.), who did not want his name mentioned, urged me to complete the quest I was then feverishly pursuing during my adolescence to the point of creating various esoteric circles, by applying to a Masonic lodge, which I did during my military service.

No one knew exactly who this first initiator was that the Grand Master of a Sufi Masonic obedience called "the Green." The second initiator of my Masonic journey, Jean Montezer, an officer of the Foreign Legion, was responsible for an obedience that had an initiatory praxis based on daily exercises. This obedience, SOFA, from the Middle East, also welcomed me the same year in Nice, a few days after my initiation in a Toulon lodge where I was sponsored by the Past Master, an Armenian highly prized for his wisdom and his inner calm acquired in his craft of upholstering who came from an Eastern brotherhood; he was therefore the third brother who contributed to my understanding of the Masonic Orders. Brother Nemo, even in the most convivial moments, when I happened to visit him in Monaco, never allowed me an absence. Some would have found him scarcely fraternal; in fact, he had the hardness of those who want to lead uncompromisingly on the path of enlightenment. Triumph and disaster, those two impostors, as Rudyard Kipling wrote—he strictly recalled me to vigilance. Later, in a so-called regular lodge, I also saw in many other brothers this quest for the way of awakening. All this is to recall that Freemasonry, as Rémi Boyer develops in his essay, is a traditional initiatory order that teachers of enlightenment attended and recommended. Then followed the dark hours when the sinister politics of the supporters of resentment took hold of certain obediences, while others were preoccupied with business, with the inevitable consequences: total ignorance of the traditional spirit, and worse still, its negation.

If the Blue Lodges were to lead to enlightenment, the Lodges of Perfection, wrongly called superior, concerned the brothers who could remove social preoccupations to deepen the Tradition. Its purpose, as I see it, is not to develop the role of the inner grades. Their goal, rather, was to discover Perfect Nature. According to Henri Corbin, Socrates would have said: "One calls Perfect Nature the sun of the philosopher"... It is the spiritual entity (the Angel) who governs it, opens the locks of wisdom, teaches that which is difficult for him, reveals to him what is right, suggests to him what the keys of the doors are, during sleep just as in the waking state. To be understood here is the intimate celebration of a personal religion, the inner dimensions of the vertical.

At a meeting of international obediences, held this year in Monte Carlo, I was surprised to see after my position statement, sister and brother delegates from various lodges and obediences arose to show their agreement. There is no doubt that Rémi Boyer's book would have been appreciated that day, because people came to ask me if there was a textbook that defined the Masonic praxis.

This is all to emphasize the valuable work which this book advocates. It follows the way of these awakeners, without being destabilized by fashions or quarrels, standing in the middle of the ruins, beyond praise and criticism, holding the torch of Tradition that does not exclude the heat and light of the heart; on the contrary! I can behold it in difficult times.

Let us hope that future Masons and those who, admitted to the Order, try to discover its essence, find in this book the keys to their inner realization, their freedom, and perhaps a day of enlightenment.

Here and now.

J.-P. de C. B.
2006

Preface to the Second Edition
By Serge Caillet

Against gentrification

"Unlike teachings based in Knowledge, Rémi Boyer questions the relevance, not [...] of occultism and theosophy, but of the traditional systems that sort these groups in relation to awakening. No man of experience can fail to approve and share his mistrust: these systems suffer, in fact, a natural tendency to confinement and this trend naturally responds to the tendency of humans to self-confinement." How can I not agree with these words of Robert Amadou, our awakener and common watcher, of eternal memory?

Against the natural confinement which traditional Freemasonry cannot escape, Rémi Boyer launched in 2006 this manifesto, in the form of a manual, for *Freemasonry as a Way of Awakening: An Essay for Pragmatic Masonic and Post-Masonic Initiation,* reissued in 2012 under the title: *Freemasonry, a Living Spirituality.*[5] A manifesto that is part of a triptych, inseparable from the other two components that are *Mask, Cloak, Silence: Martinism as a Way of Awakening* and *Beneath the Veil of Elias Artista: The Rose-Croix as a Way of Awakening, an Oral Tradition.*

---

5 The English language edition adopts the title of the first French edition.—Trans.

As for Freemasonry, the time is confusing, wrote Rémi Boyer in 2006, which current news also confirms, because confusion is permanent in the world of form. Why would Freemasonry escape from that in its varied social forms? All the more so because it is often concerned, wrongly, with the affairs of the world.

When confusion reigns, it is necessary to begin by restoring fundamental truths, even if it means pushing against open doors. Let us recall, then, that the initiatory vocation of Freemasonry requires, first of all, respect for the moral law. To a great scholar, an old mason, a man of honor, and a man of God, who admitted me to the office of Junior Warden, which I preferred among all the duties of the lodge, I once asked: what do you teach to your apprentices? And, against all odds, the wise man answered me gravely: "I teach them to be less bastardly than the others!" The point of initiation, the point of initiatory society, the point of the initiate comes out of the foundations of moral law, where beneficence, the fundamental virtue of the Mason, according to Jean-Baptiste Willermoz in particular, is essential, toward others as toward oneself. However, the excessive opening of Masonry in the world, the unrestrained competition of obediences and their outrageous recruitment can only favor, as the Masons say, "profane behavior" and the contamination of the basket by rotten fruit. For some time now, the results of these toxic effects, at all levels of the hierarchical scale, often confused with the initiatory scale, have been obvious and appalling.

The second truth first: the initiatory vocation of Masonry also implies—who knows? who says so? who cares?—the break with contemporary ideologies, starting with rationality, of Western origin, which has now won over the entire planet. We live in the time of the idolatry of reason, Karl von Eckhartshausen said indignantly in the Age of Enlightenment. What would he have said of ours!

Initiatory, it means indeed: priority to the imagination, the fertile and fertilizing imagination as opposed to mutilated and degrading reason. Priority and solidarity to the fraternity of beings (and everything in being), against the loneliness, negativity and aggressiveness that are characteristic of the modern world of ethnocide and the paths of emptiness denounced by Robert Jaulin. Priority to life, simply, against death. It is true that speculative Freemasonry, as they say, is sociologically a bourgeois phenomenon. Nevertheless, the sometimes cartoonish gentrification of Masonry, its travesty, and its adherence to political conformity and commercial conservatism are deeply anti-Masonic, because they are anti-initiatory.

Beyond reform, the Illuminist Masons, in principle, unceasingly propose to restore in Masonry "a style of existence in agreement with the universe" (Robert Amadou). However, this style of existence, in terms of social and political laws, can only severely shake up the established cultural order. Including, of course, the order established by most Masons themselves, within and outside Masonry.

In the margins, the center

Although it encourages perfection, Masonry remains an offshoot school (Pierre de Joux), because it belongs to a kind of order that is not that of accomplished initiates. These are gathered forever in the Inner Church (Lopukhin and Eckhartshausen), which is also the informal and timeless society, all spiritual (therefore without premises, without ceremony, without assembly) and all internal, the Independents or Solitaries (Louis-Claude de Saint-Martin), who are also silent and invisible, or even initiated in the wild state.

In 1972, after having assigned to Freemasonry a vocation of cultural subversion, Robert Amadou wondered: "Who can say what the effect would be in the Masonic order of a contamination of nominal initiates by initiates in the wild state? It would perhaps lead to true initiates, capable of contaminating secular society and of introducing the seeds of nonviolent subversion for the benefit of the true 'moral law'; to affirming others, not to the refusal of the other, man or culture, being or object."

With a long experience of initiation, in and out of the Masonic environment, Rémi Boyer has written a manual of this contamination, this nonviolent subversion. Distinguishing (since it is necessary to distinguish the forms) exoteric or external secret societies, mesoteric or intermediate, and esoteric or internal and refuting the term "initiatory society," applied to Masonry as to many other schools, Rémi Boyer proposes to substitute the term "societies of initiatables." But is Freemasonry a society of initiatables? The answer, frankly, is no! Whether traditional or so-called "liberal," regular or committed to the "substituted way" (Jean Baylot), it is not more so today than in the eighteenth century that saw it born, a few decades before Martinez de Pasqually denounced its apocryphal character.

A *Catechism of the Élus Coëns of the Universe,* from 1770, further distinguishes the five kinds of philosophies then in use in the Masonic world: the symbolic philosophy, which helps to "get closer to the mysterious knowledge that the Great Architect employed in the construction of the universal temple which he himself constructed by his own word," the theoretical philosophy, which "demonstrates the symbols which are analogous to the mysteries which the Great Architect employed," the practical philosophy, which "teaches to raise buildings on their bases, both spiritual and material," the composite philosophy, which "teaches the various orders that have been in the various nations of the whole world, their prevarication, their remission and their expulsion by order of the Great Architect," and, finally, apocryphal philosophy, which teaches "nothing that can be analogous to true philosophy."

Concretely, today as yesterday, the five philosophies intertwine and coexist in many social forms of the Masonic microcosm. Moreover, Freemasonry has not escaped, as we all know, from all the dysfunctions of initiatory societies as a whole. Finally, let us remember this other evidence: "Institutions sometimes serve to mitigate the ills of man, more often to increase them, never to cure them" (Saint-Martin). We must take care, therefore, not to confuse the initiatory societies, or societies of initiatables, with the initiatory ways themselves, nor the way with the more or less suitable vehicles that allow us to appropriate it. This manual of initiatory psychology will help, because it informs and disturbs, when it shows, lucidly, the rut that some, in the kingdom of the blind, confuse with the right way.

Rémi Boyer assigns to Freemasonry a very high ambition, certainly higher than the latter as such proposes, and higher than most Masons envision. This visionary Freemasonry (but it is a waking dream and a dream for awakening) which sometimes borders on utopia, or on the ideal, is it still Freemasonry? I affirm, from experience, that it is, for the small number of brothers and sisters who have chosen the occultist or mystic form, or Illuminist, as they sometimes say. Illuminist and illuminating.

Since the eighteenth century, Freemasons have indeed found in their order the opportunity to cultivate esotericism in the form of specific rites, which are related, not formally or historically, but ideally, to Hermetism, for example, or to the Rose-Croix, or to Egypt. For these, occultism or esotericism, which culminates in theosophy, is essential and vital, otherwise Masonry escapes its initiatory vocation. But occultism is inherent in all traditional culture—and ours is the only one that is no longer so—where man, says Servier, does not consider himself cut off from the Invisible and nature, but is inscribed, on the contrary, in the harmony of the relations between God, man, and the universe.

The Masonic tradition thus understood, the Masonic initiation thus lived by this connection to desire and the effectiveness of the rites, allows or should allow some to realize this desire, which is fundamentally the desire of God, that is to say the desire of the man in search of God. The Masonic fringe, which embodies this desire (often in a chaotic manner, it is true, but that does not matter) is only marginal to profane or semi-profane eyes. Invert the perspective, turn back the distorting mirror: then, the margin becomes the center.

Sometimes despised, sometimes denied, more often still unknown by their brothers, Martinez de Pasqually, Cagliostro, Saint-Martin, Willermoz, Gerard Encausse/Papus (*Ce que doit savoir un maître maçon*, 1910), Jean Bricaud, Constant Chevillon (*Le vrai visage de la franc-maçonnerie*, 1939), Robert Ambelain (*La scala philosophorum ou la symbolique des outils dans l'art royal*, 1965) and Robert Amadou (*La Tradition maçonnique*, 1986), between other human expositions of the libertarian and liberating current, showed that another way was possible. Narrow, full of pitfalls, of course. But possible.

Rites, what are they for?

They are viable, provided that they are operative. But with what tools?

Every well-known initiatory society, beginning with Freemasonry, offers initiation to man. But which man? "Those who speak of initiatory (or metaphysical) *realization* most often forget to specify *Who* realizes. Man—being metaphysically unreal—cannot *realize* reality, but only *contemplate* it," says Jean d'Encausse, at the end of his unjustly forgotten little treatise *La Philosophie de l'éveil* (1978). Initiation is not addressed to man in his original state of perfection, but to that degraded, fallen child, for whom contemplation remains the essential means of participating in the Invisible or the Real.

Since Freemasonry is a school, drawing its members from darkness to light, it thus needs a method, which the ritual proposes through symbols and rites, indissociable from myths as Mircea Eliade has shown, that are so inherent in the human condition that they persist even when all sense of the sacred seems to have disappeared, and they are so essential to Freemasonry that no one has yet managed to drive them out of the more progressive lodges.

Now, the symbolism that characterizes Freemasonry is, like all symbolism, a Gnostic process (Gilbert Durand), that is to say, an experimental knowledge of oneself, of others, of the world, and of God. But beware! This gnosis is not reduced to an ideology, it was deemed Masonic. And these symbols are not only allegories to be commented on in mediocre drawings inspired by authorized textbooks; they designate metaphysical realities, to experience onsite. A building site where, works open to the glory of the Great Architect of the Universe, who is God, all action engages all the planes of existence, which are themselves in relation with the divine world, with the invisible world, and with the natural world. Noachism thus lays the foundations of Masonry, whose ritual construction is symbolically linked to Noah, with whom the Eternal God of Life contracted the first covenant, with respect for the living, through the sacrament of the rainbow.

"The rite is not just something that signifies, it's something that works" (Jean Daniélou). If rites are effective, it is because energy is acting. Not that it is everywhere and always the same energy, but the true symbols are always effective to make men better, because they convey the Ideas (Plato), which are living beings (Villiers de l'Isle-Adam), whose contemplation persuades that the Real is elsewhere and lights the routes to it.

The rite also acts through the effect of universal correspondences, universal interdependence (Raymond Abellio) or universal sympathy, which the Greek tradition calls *suntateia*. This involves analogical interactions between things, between beings, between worlds, and the love of the Invisible (God, the gods or angels, and even the spirits, the elements...), in which the respect for nature participates.

Expression of a fundamental dimension of human existence (Jean Daniélou), rites are inseparable from man and consequently from the man of desire who is the initiatable, and from the new man who is the initiate, proceeding toward the spirit-man. Rites are the Mason's tools, which their practice makes into sacred action; rites are the tools of a sacralization of the fundamental moments of existence. If the rite is proper to life, however, it also happens that excessive formalism and misuse cut it off from its roots and condemn it to death.

Of Masonic ritual, Rémi Boyer himself offers an uncommon interpretation, for awakening. Scholars may be offended. But the alchemical interpretation of the cathedrals (Fulcanelli), the ancient myths (Michael Maïer and Dom Pernety), the metaphysical reading of fairy tales (Jean Borella), even the "initiatory" or "esoteric" interpretation of the graphic novels of *Tintin*, are not, in themselves, illegitimate, provided that one does not misunderstand the probable unconsciousness of the authors of these original works. In the same way, why would the Masonic ritual not be susceptible to a reading, a re-reading in truth, which, without necessarily being in conformity with the conscious intentions of its editors, would vivify it in the renewed initiatory spirit, against the letter that kills. Against death, in short, for life, for awakening.

The rite is neither to exaggerate nor to proscribe; it is to be sublimated, because our temporal acts need to revitalize themselves in eternity.

Initiation itself

At the beginning of the millennium, where does one look for initiation? Initiatory societies, societies of initiatables if we follow Rémi Boyer, can help. Freemasonry can help (as it can, undoubtedly, divert). But help what? Help to descend or climb (it's a matter of perspective) in oneself.

The Lesson of Saint-Martin, the Unknown Philosopher and exemplary Mason, despite his estrangement from forms: "The only initiation I seek with all the ardor of my soul is that by which we can enter the heart of God and make the heart of God enter into us, to create an indissoluble marriage, which makes us the friend, the brother, and the husband of our Divine Repairer. There is no other mystery to arrive at this holy initiation than to sink more and more into the depths of our being and not to let go till we can bring forth the living and life-giving root, because then all the fruits that we were to bear according to our kind naturally occur in us and out of us, as we see that this happens to our terrestrial trees, because they are adherents to their particular root and incessantly draw in their sap."

But, to descend into oneself, is it not first necessary to approach nature? the elements? the other, who becomes Thou, because he is also me? And the angel, our celestial prototype, which is also, according to Martinez de Pasqually, our true neighbor to love as oneself.

Tradition is transmission, we read everywhere. But of what? The point of initiation is without initiator, and it is the lodge which makes it function. It is the lodge that transmits, which receives as such the authentic sons of light (Pierre Mariel). Tradition is what is received, the real memory, and it is the light that is restored, the lost light, which is the spirit, the bearer of the Spirit. There is no other reality than this: make room for the Spirit, exhorts the Unknown Philosopher.

How is room made for the Spirit who is already there? By erasure. To be erased is to enter all initiation (Louis Pauwels), because, if the initiation consists in receiving, this reception requires beforehand the stripping out of the old man. The stripping reveals the center. Modern physics teaches us that the cosmos has no center, but the cosmos is the world of the fall of which the man was the vivifying center. For the initiate, on the other hand, the universe is always centered, because the center is absolutely constitutive of the human mind, which allows the orientation, that is to say the determination of the orient from which all the other directions of space, and consequently of the sacred space, are conceived. Determining the center determines the way.

But the center, the center of the world, where the king of the world resides (René Guénon), the type of the accomplished initiate, who is priest and king, this center is multiple. Where, instead, the unique center is incarnated in the multitude of sacred and holy places, permanent in history, that is the time and space of humanity. The story passes, the shrines remain, sublimated, or in the degenerate and degrading form of tourist attractions. But here initiatory societies are also sanctuaries, even if they are degenerate, even if they would be transformed into commercial societies and tourist attractions. Such as, too often, is Freemasonry.

"Freemasonry, what's the point?" Even as Robert Amadou bestowed, some forty years ago, such a title to a disturbing study, provocative as it was, Rémi Boyer is right to propose today an answer just as impertinent, therefore equally relevant: Freemasonry, a living spirituality.

S. C.
July 2011

Warning

> "Nothing is false that is true; nothing is true that is false. Everything is the opposite of dreams, of deceit."
> ISIDORE DUCASSE—Comte de Lautréamont. *Poems II.*

WE OBSERVE THAT THERE ARE a large number of "initiatory societies" around the world. In reality, there is no truly initiatory society, for no human creation could actually be initiatory. On the other hand, there are initiatory ways. They have their source in our own essential nature which, for a time, always a very short time, can use an initiatory society as a vessel.

Could our "initiatory societies" be "societies of initiates"? Some claim that "the initiate" does not manifest any need for society. The initiate is in fact autonomous, from the Greek *autosnomos,* "he who gives himself his own law."

No, it would be more interesting to consider our "initiatory societies" as "societies of initiatables."

Freemasonry, which Martinez de Pasqually considered apocryphal two centuries ago, is it a society of initiates? In almost all cases, we are obliged to conclude in the negative. Having become a profane society, incapable of ascesis and praxis, plagued by entrepreneurial and political (or, more simply, bourgeois[6]) concerns,

---

6   According to Emmanuel Mounier, the bourgeoisie is characterized by a particular state of mind. "Bourgeois" is one who is afraid of losing something. A tramp might be bourgeois, a prince might not be.

Freemasonry is distinguished only by a ceremonial, meaningless for most participants and assistants, from the many clubs, circles, and associations that animate modern societies.

This book proposes a methodology to serve the implementation of the pre-initiation function, a methodology that is aimed at both the candidates for initiation and the executives of societies and orders who want to "transmit" the initiation, even if we will see further on how much the idea of transmission is erroneous concerning initiation.

Finally, we warn the reader that everything that is stated here is totally false or, more exactly, everything that is stated here, like any theoretical statement, is neither true nor false, but is born from experimentation in several Masonic and Paramasonic lodges in Europe, Africa, and America. All that is presented in its pages may be useful to the committed quester.

I Of Initiation...[7]

FROM THE OUTSET, LET'S STATE THE PARADOX. Initiation is not thought of, it manifests itself, it is realized, outside of all linearity conducive to thought in which the person derealizes himself. Initiation is "unstoppable" only in a state of non-thought. Silence is required. The more the literature devotes pages to the subject, the more the so-called initiatory orders multiply and the less they encounter, not only "initiates," but the "initiatables," who themselves are rare. Time is confusing while the initiatory ushers in fusion with Being.

Initiation is by nature indefinable, elusive as the Spirit. Always, it is an initiation to one's own original nature or ultimate reality, to the Real, to the Absolute, to the Divine, to what remains, no matter the words since, precisely "there," there are no words.

However, is it possible to approach by words, if not Initiation in itself, the initiatory, the human tension toward the "more than human," that is to say the unconditioned? The concept of initiation could then perhaps give us the inkling or the intuition of the initiatory which is at the same time mystical, esoteric, and poetic and help us to define the initiatory approach with a view to the

---

7   This text was published for the first time, in a shorter version, in the first issue of the new series of the journal *Supérieur Inconnu,* the very beautiful and audacious avant-garde magazine directed by Sarane Alexandrian.

elaboration of a practice of initiation that is sorely lacking in the West. Remember, however, that everything written here is totally false or rather, is neither true nor false. Some of these lines may be useful to the sagacious mind that wants to attempt the adventure of the quest, the only adventure that is worthwhile, but the essential will be between the lines, between the words, between the letters, in the Interval.

Science, art, and initiation pose the same question *a priori:* Why is there something rather than nothing? While science tries to answer by investigating the "Thing," by probing it *in abstracto* ("Science does not prove, it probes" warns the philosopher Bateson), art deflects or exalts it better to interrogate *in facto,* sometimes even desperately, while initiation answers the question by erasing it in the full experience of the Great Nothing. Science and initiation have in common rigor, nothing more; art and initiation share nothing less than controlled madness, madness that allows the overcoming of the limits of the conditioned person.

It happens that in the earth or heaven of Tradition, four degrees of initiation are presented. The quest can indeed be arranged as follows:

I can grasp, totally and immediately, that I am the Absolute or, more precisely, "I" is grasped by the Absolute and all is over, there is nothing to do, to be—and not even that—is enough. Nothing prepares for this definitive experience, no school, no training. It is an accident or a grace of the Real.

I do not grasp the Absolute but I sense it through the perception of the divine game of energy and consciousness. I then learn to master this game by abandoning any claim to control it, to become a free creator available for the experience of the Absolute.

I do not perceive the game of energy and consciousness, so I respect and practice the rites, integrate the symbolism, and study the formal education that accompanies it.

I do not perceive the meaning of the ritual in ceremonial, so I am dedicated to improving the society in which I live and the improvement of the human being.

In each of its variations, corresponding to particular traditional expressions that we often call secret societies or initiatory orders, they assume, with more or less aptness, functions that are exoteric, mesoteric, or esoteric. It is important to distinguish formal organizations, always human and therefore conditioned, functions, which indicate processes, and ways, "non-human" and unconditioned.

An organization is always inscribed in a time, a space, and a culture. These "data" are unavoidable and clearly condition the form that the initiatory society will take. Like any organization, an initiatory society, conceived ideally to serve the liberation of the human being and to accompany the initiatory process of individuals and groups, can become a new prison. Gradually, the initiatory object will be abandoned for a totally different purpose, to perpetuate the organization, to extend its influence, to develop its power. If there is a profanation, it is this one, the shift from the initiatory to the political, the sacrifice of the quest of Being in favor of having and doing, the abandonment of verticality in favor of gaining territory or power. An initiatory society is at the service of its members, not the other way round, who must not hesitate to extract the best and then abandon it to pursue the question elsewhere and otherwise.

In the Kali Yuga, societies congeal and degenerate very quickly. It would be healthy and wise for them not to survive their founders, for the best students of these societies to found their own organization, itself ephemeral.

Formally, traditions agree on distinguishing between three types of traditional organizations, external, semi-internal, and internal. Let's quickly see what this distinction is, which is independent of the nature and purpose of the organization.

An attempt at a functional typology of initiatory societies can help us to think of a universal phenomenon present since ancient times in almost all cultures.

Secret societies assume three particular functions, both distinct and complementary, which we call exoteric, mesoteric—or sometimes exo-esoteric, and esoteric.

The exoteric function is primarily of a therapeutic nature. It aims to restore the individual alignment, the congruence, between body, emotion, and thought. It is important to reconcile the person with self and environment. This function implies a certain cultural component since the person is invited to study, meditate, and if possible integrate, a model of the world, qualified as spiritual, that allows him to find an answer satisfactory to the mind and reassuring to the heart, in relation to the big problems that life keeps asking him. This function, important for the individual who benefits from it, is also socially regulative. By helping the individual to find a balance in the world as it is, secret societies of this type promote the stability and slow evolution of the dominant political, economic, and social systems. Freemasonry today perfectly illustrates this last point. In periods of tension, they are, on the contrary, vectors of change in society. Think of the Cosmic Movement in Russia which was a hotbed for revolutionary ideas. External secret societies (but then can we still speak of secret societies?) generally assume this exoteric function alone, even though they often claim to assume a more esoteric function. Note that sometimes, on the contrary, depending on the context and the politics of the obedience, they defend themselves from any esotericism thus demonstrating their radical removal from any initiatory virtue. With René Girard, remember that a scandal is an obstacle that irresistibly attracts. This is enantiodromic behavior[8] following the strange interdependence of opposites already noted by Heraclitus.

The mesoteric function should be assumed by societies, less numerous and more closed than the previous ones, already constituted in true traditional schools. They strive to give their students the basic skills needed to claim an approach to a real way. These qualifications may vary according to the currents of the traditions. Thus in the Rosicrucian current, knowledge and mastery of the "high sciences" of the *Trivium Hermeticum* will be required, namely alchemy, astrology, and magic. But independently of the corpus and the proposed operativities,[9] two technical imperatives will characterize this function and will invariably be found in all organizations of this type, because they condition the reality of the operativities:

The experimentation of the universe is viewed as "answer" to an "absolutely" oriented will. To obtain the answer of the universe is indeed the quality, the definition if one believes Giordano Bruno, of the Mage, the one who is will, who makes the universe answer. This is not of course the personal will, the fruit of desire, but the creative desire of the Being born in Silence.

The search for the objective state. In order to illustrate what we mean by objective state and awakening, we will cite here Ouspensky:[10]

---

8   Enantiodromic: that which is reversed or transformed into its opposite (Heraclitus).

9   Operativity (French, *opérativité*): in this context, a way of work with an internal or esoteric component (e.g., alchemy, divination, ritual, etc.).—Trans.

10   P.D. Ouspensky, *In Search of the Miraculous* (London: Routledge & Kegan Paul, 1950), pp. 141-142.

> The third state of consciousness is **self-remembering** or self-consciousness or consciousness of one's being. It is usual to consider that we have this state of consciousness or that we can have it if we want it. Our science and philosophy have overlooked the fact that we **do not possess** this state of consciousness and that we cannot create it in ourselves by desire or decision alone.
>
> The fourth state of consciousness is called the **objective state of consciousness.** In this state a man can see things as they are. Flashes of this state of consciousness also occur in man. In the religions of all nations there are indications of the possibility of a state of consciousness of this kind which is called "enlightenment" and various other names but which cannot be described in words. But the only right way to objective consciousness is through the development of self-consciousness. If an ordinary man is artificially brought into a state of objective consciousness and afterwards brought back to his usual state he will remember nothing and he will think that for a time he had lost consciousness. But in the state of self-consciousness a man can have flashes of objective consciousness and remember them.
>
> The fourth state of consciousness in man means an altogether different state of being; it is the result of inner growth and of long and difficult work on oneself.
>
> But the third state of consciousness constitutes the natural right of man **as he is,** and if man does not possess it, it is only because of the wrong conditions of his life. It can be said without any exaggeration that at the present time the third state of consciousness occurs in man only in the form of very rare flashes and that it can be made more or less permanent in him only by means of special training.
>
> For most people, even for educated and thinking people, the chief obstacle in the way of acquiring self-consciousness consists in the fact that **they think they possess it**...

This reference to a central state of being, to an axis of the world, to a Kingdom of the Center is common to all traditions. Its importance is considerable, technically and practically. Thus, the Master Mason is received in the Middle Chamber, referring to a Kingdom of the Center, accessible only to the one who can stop thinking of the universe through the game of multiple representations in order to perceive the Universe, to leave the diluting world of having and doing for that of Being. The process of self-remembering causes a destruction of mental identifications and crystallizations, and consequently the beliefs that underlie the profane personality, the *Persona*, the mask, will be destroyed during this quest of Being. Few are ready to lose the images they have of themselves and of the world, the products of their multiple conditionings, the source of their sufferings, but also of some ephemeral pleasures.

While the exoteric schools are aimed at the person and seek to satisfy the needs of belonging and recognition, the mesoteric societies gradually discard the person in order to leave room for the Being. It is not in the personal field that the operativities can be implemented but in the zone of silence, in the unconditioned. Then, the operative truly becomes art, and the operator, free of any need and any search for result, operates for the beauty and joy of the gesture itself.

The esoteric function should concern, let us repeat, only autonomous beings. *Autosnomos* means, "he who gives himself his own law." It means going outside of the circle of identifications, dilutions, representations, and mental crystallizations, to reach the Center where simply "I am" or "I remain." No longer "to be lived," but to live. It is only in the Center that one can give oneself to one's law, to be autonomous. It is only through the Center, the Axis of Being, that Theurgy and Alchemy can be realized. Probably, the qualifier of *initiatory* should be reserved for the esoteric function. We do not use the word *esotericism* as a generic term for the nebula of movements that deal with spirituality, hermeticism, or occultism, but specifically to distinguish between what concerns the unspeakable and the incommunicable, of what can only be accessed through direct experience. The truly esoteric societies, most often collegiate, are conceived as true research laboratories. They lead their followers into the terminal phases of the Real Paths, the Way of Awakening, the Way of the Body of Glory, the Way of the Red Stone, the Essential Way, the Extreme Way, the names are numerous to designate this phase where the individual released from all that is human, liberated even from the liberation, accesses in a real way conscious immortality and becomes a god, compared to his former state of humanity. At this point, it is almost out of place to talk about organizations, or societies, which are mere human creations. The terms Assembly (*Ekklesia*) or *Ordo* in the priestly sense of the term would be more adequate. The true internal orders are for the most part "floating" structures that come and go, appear here and there, move easily from one form to another. They have integrated impermanence as a structural mode of operation. In reality, there are no truly esoteric schools, but Lines in which the relationship between the master (the one who masters the art and the discipline and who can be a collective) and the student or the disciple (the one who applies the discipline to achieve the art), constitutes the basis of this terminal and very internal work. The names of these lineages, assemblies, and "serpentine" orders appear and disappear, are rarely pronounced and remain unknown, even to historians of esotericism.

In some cases, less rare than is supposed, the Lines, vehicles of the secret ways, are preserved in family traditions, often families of aristocrats or the religious, but not necessarily and less and less. The family conceived as an initiatory school is indeed a very traditional concept. Thus the Indian master Krishnamacharya, custodian of the Indian Pythagorean lineage, developed a whole teaching aimed at making the family an esoteric school. In Italy, aristocratic families from Venice or Florence were the repositories of an initiatory secret. Villiers de l'Isle Adam speaks about it explicitly in his key novel *Isis*. Even today, it is only in the restricted circle of the family, sometimes extended to a few close friends, that for technical reasons, certain operativities can be practiced just as, in the past or in antiquity, was the case in khan families or pharaonic families.

The distinction of initiatory societies into three functions and in three forms is very classic. We find it for example in the work of Fernando Pessoa. In *Le Chemin du Serpent*, Pessoa distinguishes three orders: an *Ordo Serpentes*, an *Ordo Solis*, and an *Ordo Sebastica*, which would be "occult and without exterior." However, by examining this double categorization, external, semi-internal, internal, and exoteric, mesoteric, and esoteric, it is easy to fall into the mainstream of asserting that external societies assume the exoteric function, semi-internal societies the mesoteric function, and internal societies the esoteric function. It would be reassuring to put some here and others there, especially since it would not be totally wrong. Thus Masonic obediences, the many Rosicrucian organizations, and the Martinist orders would be in their place in the exoteric external societies with a distinction of size: Masonic obediences serve as a breeding ground for semi-internal societies while Martinist orders serve as a platform where researchers from different horizons meet collectively. Both are not just that, of course. We would rank in the second group orders like the Templar and Magical Fraternity of Myriam, the Order of the Golden Dawn, the various Pythagorean Orders, the Kabbalistic Order of the Rose-Croix, the Order of the Rose-Croix of the Orient, among others, and even some specific Masonic obediences such as the Italian Philosophical Rite or the

Great Adriatic Sanctuary. And even a few names would come to haunt the third category such as the Order of Osiris, the Order of Mantos, the Order of the Initiated Brothers of Asia, the Hermetic Brotherhood of Luxor, or the Order of the Golden Rosy-Cross of the Ancient System. It would be to forget the unpredictable and absolutely libertarian character of the quest and the uncertainty of human constructions.

It seems important to prioritize the initiatory way over the organization, whatever it is, the latter being only the dressing or the very momentary vehicle of the former. It may be relevant, then, to return to etymology to make a new distinction. The word initiation comes from the Latin *initiatio* which itself, in the Graeco-Roman period, translated the Greek word *telete*. Except, while the word *initiatio* expresses the idea of passage (scientists only retain from initiation the rite of passage), *telete* conveys the idea of completion, of accomplishment. While the *initiatio* is based on imitation and repetition, which make rites, *telete* is based on "the very liberation of liberation" according to Nikos Kazantzakis. Every path begins where imitation and repetition cease. It is an abandonment of forms, including the sacred forms that are the rites, to penetrate the Real. The initiatory approach foresees an obligatory passage, one that marks the renunciation of *imitatio,* to take the path of *inventio,* where each gesture, each breath, each moment are at the same time totally new, totally accomplished, totally unique. The accomplished *initiate* is a naked and free being, deprived and freed from all the cultural and cultured superimpositions, from all human conditioning, a being in silence, freed from language, a vehicle privileged from conditioning. The initiate has no need to name the thing. He is the thing itself. He is the game of energy and consciousness, the game without "I."

We would like to conclude with the very symbol of initiation and the most significant myth of the Western initiatory tradition, the Rosy-Cross. Constant and axis of the European hermetic scene since the seventeenth century in its multiple cultural expressions, the Rosy-Cross remains elusive as the Spirit, perhaps because its own nature is Spirit. It is, besides the most fertile creative metaphor of the Western tradition, metaphysical and a philosophy of the quest, as we would say today a metaphysical philosophy of awakening. A metaphysical philosophy that supports, as much as (after a rigorous propaedeutic) they are supported by, an ascesis, a poetry, a *tekhne,* that want to inscribe the Spirit in form to better free itself from it, possibly by a theurgy, or a metallic or internal alchemy, but not necessarily. The Rosy-Cross is sometimes only stripping to the Essence. The Temple of the Rosy-Cross is a place-state inscribed everywhere and nowhere, and the spirit of Elias Artista, the tutelary angel of the Rosy-Cross, its *Breath,* makes the quester a red monk. He is alone and complete in himself because he, autonomous, gives to himself his own law, a solitary artist of emptiness and plenitude, a master of nothing and everything who has chosen the nomadic alternative. The quest of the Rose-Christ is always unconditional and liberatory, in its way as in its orientation.

Ergon or *Parergon,* one by the other, the other by one, the Lightning of Elias Artista seals what is accomplished in *Christ, Christ* not to be here understood in his religious sense, the anointed one who connects, but in the solar sense of Absoluteness. It is always a question of being oriented toward, and nourished by, this Absolute, thus tracing the axis of Being that *Sophia* conveys, the axis around which the serpentine paths of the Real wind. These uncertain paths, which appear under the feet of the traveller and disappear behind him, settle in inevitable intervals: *Agape, Aletheia, Askesis, Eros, Ethos,* and some others to draw a higher Geometry of the Sages, a science of the Interval. This is not a path to silence, nor a silent path, it is the Silence that is on the path. Here we must understand what is technically required of self-remembering, of self-presence, of the intensity of consciousness in the great game of energy, at once a definitive answer and a call to grace. The very inspiring metaphor of the Rosy-Cross conveys the possibility of a "not yet possible" actualized in the passing moment by an ineffable Love which thus opens a new Eon. It is not a poetic formula, but a practice that is suggested here, a very lively practice, but also difficult to master and to achieve.

Last but not least, in appearance anyway, where does one look, at the beginning of this millennium, for Initiation? In itself. By itself. Even so? In Nature, in the Earth, in the spirit of the Water, in the spirit of the Air, in the Fire... In the unexpected and creative relationship maintained with the Feminine... In the artistic avant-garde... In every encounter... free from all need, far, far away from all human conventions. In Love and paradoxical Adventure.

2 The Initiatory Approach

> "Nothing is less strange than the contradictions that we discover in man. He is made to know the truth. He is in search of it. When he tries to seize it, he is dazzled and confused in such a way that no one would challenge him for it. Some want to rob man of the knowledge of the truth, others want to assure him of it. Each employs such dissimilar reasoning that they negate his perplexity. He has no other light than that which is found in his own nature."
>
> ISIDORE DUCASSE—Comte de Lautréamont. *Poems II.*

THE INITIATORY APPROACH PRESENTS inevitable steps that we will attempt to discover and analyze:

- The request for initiation
- Analysis of the request
- Passage under the blindfold
- Initiation instruction and orientation to the tradition
- The "first" initiation
- The initiatory work
- Evaluation

We will approach each of these stages within the setting of a Masonic formulation, but what will be stated will remain valid for any initiatory current having a formal aspect, that is to say comprising a ceremonial and an organization of a Masonic type. This is the case for a very large majority of Western initiatory societies.

For the other initiatory approaches, some of what will be presented here will be unfit for the understanding of the system, but it will correspond to the most formal part.

1. The request for initiation

The initiatory request, all request, is born in a context, cultural, economic, political, and personal. It is necessary to put each request in context.

On the one hand, an initiatory secret society, even a secular one, is always inscribed in a given cultural space and historical time. Its expression, subject to evolution, is linked to both history and geography. Thus initiation in a lake village does not rely on the myths that underlie a mountain initiation. The place of the secret society in its time largely determines the expectations of those who knock on its door. To ask for the light in Freemasonry in 1943 does not have the same meaning, for the applicant as well as for those to whom the request is addressed, as that at the beginning of the third millennium.

On the other hand, the person is himself a product of the hypercomplexity of the times that he has gone through and that he lives sequentially or simultaneously: sacred time, profane time, physical time, metaphysical time, biological time, personal time, etc. Its model of time and its model of space determine how it is conceived in its relation to the universe and in the construction of its own otherness. The models of time and space are largely determined by the relation to language.[11] German culture pres-

---

11 See Edward T. Hall, *Beyond Culture* (Garden City, NY: Anchor/Doubleday, 1975), *The Silent Language* (Garden City, NY: Doubleday, 1959), *The Dance of Life: The Other Dimension of Time* (Garden City, NY: Anchor/Doubleday, 1983).

ents a monochronic time[12] and a low-context language.[13] Italian culture has a polychronic time and a high context language. Both have received major initiatory currents, but their expressions are radically different except for their innermost aspects. The request for initiation will manifest itself differently in both cultures.

Whoever hears the request will themselves have to be aware of the context that has determined and accompanied their own journey, in other words, the conditions which, for the most part, have determined their own quest, in order to receive this request from a layman as it is and not as they would like it to be, a projection of their own beliefs or desires. This means that one can only hear and understand the initiation request of a layman who is deeply involved in the quest and already at a distance from his cultural and personal components, an attitude impossible to hold in the absence of rigorous praxis.

The personal, more intimate context of the applicant will also have to be taken into account. Is the person in a stable and balanced period of his life or, on the contrary, in a more eventful or painful period (loss of work, rupture, death of an intimate…)? Does she have children? The model of the world of a father or a mother will always be different, suffused with an experience incomprehensible for the one who did not live it. Age is also a determining factor. One does not knock at the door of the temple

---

[12] Concerning *Chronos,* time, E.T. Hall, who modeled the active representations of time in the psyche, distinguishes monochronic models, which see the times linked in sequence one behind the other (a time to work, a time to eat, a time to love…) and the polychronic models that present a simultaneity of times (for example, professional time can also be superimposed on private time).

[13] In a low-context language, the context in which the message is emitted and received brings little information. The message must itself contain a lot of information to be explicit. In a language with a high context, the context is already carrying a lot of information that does not have to be included in the message.

in the same way at twenty-five as at fifty, if only because the question of death, in the background of any initiatory step, is made more urgent, more conscious, as one advances in age.

Contexts are elements of desire. The layman, man of the stream, becomes a man of desire, to use the expression dear to Louis-Claude de Saint-Martin, as soon as he considers an initiatory approach. Desires are fruits largely conditioned by contexts.

The request for initiation must always be heard with respect, whoever the person is who makes it, tramp or prince, uneducated or scholar, mobster or saint, because a genuine request necessarily comes from the heart, the being in itself.

It will be during interviews that the request will first be received, then elaborated. Those who conduct the interviews will begin a valuable collection of information that will later serve to indicate and elaborate the initiatory process, but will seek to establish as soon as possible the conditions of initiation. These first moments are particularly important. They determine the quality of the work that will ensue.

The term "interview" is preferable to that (very Masonic and also very policelike) term, "investigation." The interview must be part of a real encounter and not for the sake of investigation, which does not go far beyond the surface structure of communication.

Each of these encounters follows a specific protocol: the establishment of a deep rapport—a precise collection of information—a mapping of contexts—an identification of the psychological and intellectual resources of the applicant—a clarification of the objectives—the verification of the ecology—a bridge to the future. The person conducting the interview must never lose sight of the fact that in no case, and especially if no follow-up should be given to this interview, should the layman feel worse after the meeting than before.

Let's take a brief look at each step of these meetings:

Establish a deep and respectful relationship: the interviewer will have to harmonize himself with the subject, not only with appropriate behavior, but also with the candidate's language structure and content, and, for a while, adopt his or her own values and beliefs. It is by penetrating into the model of the world of the candidate that one can best appreciate its richness and approach the meaning of the journey. Moving from the surface structure of communication to the deep structure, it will be possible to identify what the founding experiences are that led the candidate to knock on the door of a temple.

Once rapport is established, the collection of information must begin. Criteria, values, core beliefs, and secondary beliefs structure the personality. Meta-programs determine the processes that build experiences. Particular attention will be paid to how a person adopts and maintains a new belief and to the model of the person's time.

The identification of the applicant's psychological and intellectual resources is based on his experiences. Most of our resources have their origins in our childhood or indeed our infancy. Our most distant memories are carriers of unsuspected resources yet are barely conditioned by the social and cultural environment. Some resources and qualifications are needed to tackle the initiatory question. Identifying the resources in the person helps him, when the time comes, to organize them creatively. The fragility of the person is not necessarily a handicap if the resources are present and accessible.

Clarifying the candidate's objectives is not easy. The real motivations are often unconscious. However, we will seek to establish whether the objectives, conscious or not, once achieved, will meet the needs of security, belonging, recognition, or achievement of the person. Only the needs of realization are of initiatory nature. However, many people need belonging, recognition, even security, physical or psychological, before they let the needs of realization emerge in them.

Verification of the ecology is essential. If the person is accepted in the initiatory setting, what will change in his family, professional, and religious life? There is often incompatibility between the approach envisaged, the requirements of commitment and availability of the spirit, and the family or professional context. Conflicts of belief may appear, conflicts of loyalty also. The initiatory process releases conditioning and attachments, and this liberation is sometimes unbearable for one's associates. Is the applicant mindful?

A bridge to the future serves to broaden the candidate's choices. Whatever mutual decisions are made, it is always better to consider several paths. There must never be one way to look to the future. The candidate must never end up in an ultimatum situation, "that or nothing," which in case of refusal could lead to a collapse of the personality and an urge to a drastic act.

2. Analysis of the initiation request

The collection of information carried out by the persons assigned to conduct interviews or surveys must be used for an analysis of the request. The joining of the views of the three people generally assigned to this subtle exercise, in the presence of their peers—the Masters gathered in the Middle Chamber in the case of the Masonic Order—should lead to unlocking the model of the world of the candidate for initiation, his criteria, his values, his beliefs, conscious and especially unconscious, his conditioning, to predict his reactions in certain ordinary or non-ordinary situations of life.

We will thus have two anamneses, a personal anamnesis and an initiatory anamnesis. The personal history is the story of the person, the facts, but also the story that the person tells himself about the events of his life. The initiatory anamnesis is another story, linked in an unconscious or preconscious way to the history of the person. It is the story that the person tells himself about his initiatory request. How does he explain it? What is he anchoring on? It is also a series of facts that can have an initiatory echo. We sometimes meet people who already have a spiritual or initiatory history, who have gone through other traditional structures. More certainly, everyone has experiences that have an initiatory nature, in other words, that refer to Being. They can be cultural, artistic, sporting, loving, etc. It may be a drama, perhaps an innocuous event that will have led the individual to get closer to himself, to wonder deeply about meaning.

We can sometimes identify a chain of events or non-events that led the person to knock on the door. On the contrary, the request may seem without history, without sequence, without process, a lively, unexplained, unjustified emergence. The analysis of the demand is very delicate. Is this a request from the person? Is it a request from Being? Is it a request from the person in the name of Being? Is it the request from someone else, friend, family member, imaginary or historical person with whom the candidate would have identified?

The request may appear to come from the candidate but be a false request. It may seem to be dictated by a third party but correspond to a real call. The question then will be to determine, where the is demand coming from? Who speaks? This is one of the objectives, not the only one, of the passage under the blindfold.

Traditionally, we repeat that we have no right to leave a request unanswered. This does not mean to accede to the desire of the candidate but to seek with him and for him, the path most adapted to his situation. In Martinism, it is said that no one has the right to refuse initiation. But initiation is inherent in life itself. No one has the power to refuse it. On the other hand, it will be the initiator's responsibility to orient the candidate toward the group and the current that will favor a creative relationship to this vital initiation. This implies that the initiator has a strong initiatory culture, a good knowledge of the traditional scene, to make the link between the constellation of values and resources of the candidate and the configuration of an initiatory response (order, rite, lodge...).

3. *The passage under the blindfold*

Few people are aware of the importance of the passage under the blindfold. This dive into obscurity and uncertainty is in reality the first initiation, following which will be only a repetition of further and further elaboration.

The passage under the blindfold is not a sort of playful exercise so that the brothers and sisters can demonstrate, to the best of their ability, their sagacity, their humor, or the full extent of their knowledge, but a plunge conducted by the candidate into the darkness of self.

The passage under the blindfold corresponds, alchemically, to the decomposition of the raw material. To do this, it is necessary to salt and in this case, salt is the word, the language. Since language is precisely what structures the artifice of the person, superimpositions onto Being, the difficulty lies in the use of language to dissolve language. It is an art to know how to use a poison to fight against the devastating effects of this poison.

The successive questions, the interrogation of the answers, have for their first objective to lead the candidate, with elegance,[14]

---

14 Elegance must be understood as the slightest intervention causing the biggest favorable change for the candidate and the establishment of a state of consciousness conducive to initiation.

to silence, and to give him the sense of Being, of reality in itself. Those who have experienced this type of passage under the blindfold know the upheaval represented by this experience of the thrill of Being. Few lodges, Masonic or non-Masonic, in Europe, are formed for this type of work which is nevertheless the justification for the passage under the blindfold.

The second goal under the blindfold will be to clarify the request if needed and to determine what the candidate's needs are to be met. If it is the need for security that the candidate wants to satisfy, he will expect the lodge to provide him with a safe and secure space and a network in which he can integrate socially to feel that he exists. If it is the needs of recognition or belonging that are predominant, the candidate is a part of the problem of the "person" that requires a structure assuming a therapeutic or reconciling function. Finally, if it is the needs of realization which assert themselves, we are properly within an initiatory journey. However, the hypercomplexity of the human person is such that any hasty conclusion needs to be avoided. Indeed, a person who seems to manifest a bitter lack of satisfaction with his needs for security, or belonging and recognition, can, once they are satisfied, express a strong need for realization.

In sum: if the candidate is always there, under the blindfold, as a person, this tends to indicate that we are called to an exoteric, therapeutic function, that of reconciliation. If the candidate has started to take off the mask, to stand back, to position himself as a witness, we are in a call to a mesoteric function and it is not the same type of work that should be proposed to him. Finally, does the candidate become faceless? Did he agree to be unveiled under the blindfold? If this is the case, we are in an esoteric approach, an issue of awakening, and it is no longer in terms of structure that we will provide the answer, but in terms of the way.

4. Initiation instruction and orientation to the tradition

The candidate knocking on the door of a lodge is not an object but a potential subject of an initiatory process. He is not on the periphery of the concerns of the lodge but at the center of a project which aims to change him from a man of the stream to a man of desire, to be realized as being in oneself.

After the interviews with the candidate and the passage under the blindfold, the lodge must be able to answer some essential questions:

Does the request emanate from the subject? Is it not the result of the desire of a third party, often a member of the lodge?

What is the nature of the subject's needs?

What resources and skills does the subject have to engage in the initiatory venture?

What support would he need?

Are we able to offer him such support over time?

If this is not the case, to which initiatory or cultural structure can we guide him?

Too often we see the candidates being systematically received "fraternally" because, truly, it is difficult to say no to someone who asks to join an initiatory vessel. However, the indiscriminate acceptance of many members in the Masonic obediences has led to the dissolution of its initiatory character. It is the responsibility of the officers of the lodge to receive in the temple only subjects ready for the quest and who are adequate to the lodge project.

Two proposals seem to me to be needed to avoid the pitfalls of sloppiness:

The accountability of the sponsors. The godfather in initiation is not a "friend" who offers a bit of the path for viewing. He is the referent and guarantor, the referent of the subject for whom he must embody the spirit of the quest, the guarantor of the lodge he must preserve from any toxic intrusion. There are some lodges that apply a severe but justified rule: if the subject turns out to be unsuitable for the conditions of initiation to the point that the lodge must be separated from him, the sponsor agrees to leave the lodge at the same time as his godson.

The answer of the lodge to the request of the candidate must not be binary. It should never be formulated in the radical form yes/no, but in the form of a real choice. Remember that a choice requires at least three proposals. A binary choice, with two propositions, is too much like an ultimatum. Moreover, the widening of choices, behavioral and psychological, is part of initiatory applications. By proposing several possible structures of response, including possibly the lodge that studied his request, the candidate is truly recognized as the subject of the process, at the very heart of the project, the importance of which we will see later on.

5. The "first" initiation

As indicated above, the true first initiation, initiation into the Real, whatever the names by which we designate it, lies in the passage under the blindfold. We will, however, consider here the first ritual initiation by which the candidate, a layman, enters the sacred domain and dimension represented by the temple. This first initiation is particularly important as it will condition the entry of the recipient into a truly initiatory process.

Whatever the rite and the traditional current, this first ceremony has several effects:
- It profoundly modifies the model of the world of the new initiate, offering him a new setting of values, criteria, and beliefs, favorable to the entry into an operative process.
- It creates a first breach in the shackles of conditioning that constitute the "person," an interval in the continuum of history we tell ourselves in order to have the feeling of existence.

- It creates a cleavage in the unity of the person, an artificial but technically effective cleavage between the profane person and the sacred person. From now on, there is an inside and an outside, a secular space and a sacred space, a secular time and a sacred time. Later, when the person has freed up the space for Being, the initiate will be fully aware that this opposition, like any opposition, has no basis. But for the time being this cleavage, reinforced by the practices of remembering oneself and presence, will allow us to gradually adopt an initiatory posture that radically refutes the imposture of the person or the self.

It turns out that even a ritual done in a theatrical way, without expanded awareness of the stakes, is likely to trigger these three essential effects in the hopes of the effectiveness of praxis and integration of the corresponding traditional corpus.

6. *The initiatory work*

Praxis and corpus constitute the two great pillars of initiatory work. It goes without saying that in almost all orders that claim to be initiatory and especially in Freemasonry, neither praxis nor corpora are proposed. It is necessary to question this drift which makes it more likely that the most "lazy" and "idiotic" of monks will have approached the center of his Being, his own reality, than a sincere, intelligent, and cultivated Freemason.

Instruction should not be reduced to an introduction to symbolism, even if brilliant. It must offer a real corpus for study and a precise and proven program of psycho-physiological exercises that all aim to silence the mind, to give access to silence, to remember oneself in an ever-increasing awareness, to prepare for mastery.

If, in Freemasonry, the Master Mason is received in the Middle Chamber, it indicates the exit of the multiple peripheries of representations, the state of presence, at midday as at midnight, on the axis of the real, inscribed in the verticality of Being and no longer a prisoner of the stubborn threads of mental representations born of doing and having.

We will return later to the nature of this work. For the moment, it is important to understand that in the absence of such training, the conditions created by the ceremonial and the rite at the first initiation will quickly fade, that the secular/sacred break erodes in favor of an invasion of the profane, that the person will recompose around a new story including the recent experience caused by the initiation, develop new defenses, even more active, against the experience of Being and therefore, it will be even more difficult for the recipient to resume a true initiatory path later, since he will be persuaded, wrongly, that he is already an "initiate."

7. The evaluation

The initiatory work must be open to self-evaluation and evaluation regarding the subject, in order to adjust exercises and studies, to propose necessary pauses, thus respecting the initiatory breath, in the form of travels, special meetings, or different studies, or to consider another orient or another way. This implies a shared trust between the practitioner and the instructor, between the individual and the lodge.

It is not the person who is evaluated but the work, especially that of initiation. It is the erasure of the person concerned, leaving room for Being. Three areas can serve as vectors for this evaluation: the control of the internal dialogue or thoughts, the relation to the emotions, and the behavior.

I have already given elsewhere elements of verification of the correctness of a practice.[15] Measuring the relevance of a real

---

15 Rémi Boyer, *Mask Cloak Silence: Martinism as a Way of Awakening* (Bayonne, NJ: Rose Circle, 2021), pp. 153–171.

practice is primarily behavioral. Mastery of the environment, the art of "bending" time, development of energy and *solitude,* and greater serenity, are some of the observable changes. Attention, emptiness, mastery of creative power, and emotional freedom are other criteria which we cannot fake. The autonomy that results from real practice is manifested in all areas of life, social, family, professional, sports, etc. A work that does not generate significant changes is either inappropriate for the subject, or is personal development and not initiation. Confusion is common.

This appreciation of the effects of work in the fields of energy, consciousness, and the relation to time is indispensable for the subject to be able to determine and trace the path that will lead him to his own reality. Gradually, the instructor and the lodge will be only the companion, the friend of the high country of the spirit, the subject being always the best expert of his own accomplishment.

3 The Initiatory Work, Project, and Setting

> "Sleep is a reward for some, a torment for others. For all, it is a sanction."
>
> ISIDORE DUCASSE—Comte de Lautréamont. *Poems II.*

The two great functions of initiatory work

Initiatory work has two main functions: a restorative function and an awakening function. The restorative function is manifested by the ritual. It is supported by the setting, and guaranteed by the order or the rite. The awakening function is conveyed by practices, supported by the process, and guaranteed by the setting.

The restorative function involves two attitudes and two skills. The member, the brother or the sister, must be capable of alliance with the doctrine. The doctrine still exists even among those who guard themselves. It is, at least, inscribed and presented in the rituals. Alliance does not mean adherence or allegiance, let alone identification. Alliance means acceptance for a time of a set of beliefs that gives meaning to the practice. But the adage remains: "If the doctrine bothers you, reject the doctrine and pursue the practices." On the other hand, the subject must be capable of an alliance with the group. This alliance alone will lead him to develop a co-creativity with his fellow adventurers. A person incapable of alliance cannot enter into an initiatory structure based, even if only partially, on an initiatory community of work.

The awakening function will require the reverse skills. The subject must be able to distance himself from the doctrine and from the group, in order to become autonomous and capable of self-training, even of self-training in difficult times. Distance from doctrine makes it possible to integrate it as one means among others and not as a truth. Distance from the group develops the disposition to solitude without which no progress in the way is possible.

We see the paradox in which we find ourselves. These two functions must be present in a balanced way in the life of the lodge and the group. The vigilance of the instructors, referents, "initiators," Masters of lodges, Senior and Junior Wardens, sponsors, or others is engaged here. It is their responsibility to ensure the maintenance of the alliance and the keeping of distance. In certain phases of the life of the subject and the group, the alliance will have to be reinforced while at other times, the distance will be prioritized. We are on the edge of the sword blade and the experience—not the age—and sagacity of the referents will be decisive.

The initial time will be devoted to the alliance. It will be constructed by experiencing and studying rituals. So that the alliance does not lead the subject to an identification with the doctrine, the operative function of a ritual will have to be clearly explained and the uncertainties and the philosophical or cultural contradictions indicated without hesitation.

The initiatory project

The initiatory work is always part of the project. This project appears as a triptych: the project of the order or rite, the project of the lodge, and the individual project. These three aspects will have to be kept intelligently distinct from one another.

The project, presented in these three dimensions will perform two functions: a referential function and a communication function.

The implementation of this project will be organized around its axis. It can be an initiatory project, a spiritual project, a therapeutic project, or even a social project. In certain circumstances it will be necessary to return to the personal project, the project of the lodge, or the project of the order or rite to rectify the work. The project will also indicate the criteria used to evaluate the work.

The communication function fits within the dimension of connection. It is a pretext for the religious, the weaving of connections, visible and invisible, among all those who share the initiatory adventure. The communicaton function conveys the religious function without promoting religiosity.

Nested settings

Four settings fit into each other: the institutional setting, the partnership setting, the individual project setting, and the initiatory work setting.

- The institutional setting is defined by the orientation of the order or rite, the doctrine of the order, and the rules of the order as manifested by the lodge. The institutional setting has several functions. It is reassuring and comforting. It is contained, that is to say that the subject feels, internally, preserved. In this "interior," he will come to explore his own interiority and face the problems inherent in a genuine initiatory process but will also share with his brothers and sisters in the adventure.

- The partnership setting is included in the lodge contract. The lodge has made a commitment to accompany the subject who, for his part, has registered as a partner of an adventure both intellectual and spiritual. Two functions characterize the partnership setting, those of differentiation and structuring. The subject will begin to differentiate what is of the order of the profane and what is of the order of the sacred even if, from the beginning, it is clarified that this differentiation is not real but is part of the means and that later, this distinction will fade away. However, at this stage of the work, there is an exterior and there is an interior. As a general rule, the subject is either in the interior of the lodge or is exterior to the lodge, inside or outside. Metals are abandoned outside, and by metals we mean passions, defects, and mental crystallizations. Through initiatory work, it will be the "person" himself, the false entity nourished with conditionings, who will remain at the door of the temple, with only Being accessing the sacred space. The lodge contract, which can be tacit and not explicit, but is always readable, structures this adventure to which the subject is invited.
- The setting of the individual project calls for three types of alliance: an alliance with a referent, an alliance with the initiator or with the master of the lodge, and an alliance with the self. It is the practices that will gradually bring out this covenant with the Self.
- Finally, there remains the setting of the initiatory work itself. It is defined by the choice of praxis and the investment of the subject in all of the operative dimension.

If the settings are clearly laid out, if their interlocking is harmonious, the three components of the initiatory project will find an environment favorable to their realization by the order, the rite, the lodge, and the subject. The various functions that contribute to the initiation can be fully manifested and we will end up with a co-creativity of all, or at least the greatest number, for the "good of the order" according to the formula, but especially, and this is the purpose of any initiatory structure, for the realization by each of his own original and ultimate reality.

4 Space, Time, and Companionage[16]

> "In its own name, despite itself, necessarily: I come to deny, with an indomitable will and an iron tenacity, the hideous past of weeping humanity."
>
> ISIDORE DUCASSE—Comte de Lautréamont. *Poems I.*

LET'S RETURN TO THE LODGE CONTRACT, the cornerstone of initiatory orders based on the group rather than the lineage.

Space and time

What is the lodge? The lodge gathers in an in-between, a very particular space. Once assembled in the temple and the lodge having been formed, the brothers and sisters are still in the world without being really of the world. The lodge is a kind of parenthesis inside the world. A space dedicated by the will of those gathered there to finally be, for a time, themselves, or to try to approach their authentic being.

The lodge is also formed in a time apart, a different time that we call sacred, a kind of interval within the profane world, a breach in the conditioned temporality.

---

16 Companionage (French, *compagnonnage*): a guild or brotherhood in the French building trades. Often used to refer to Freemasonry, especially the membership of the Second Degree.—Trans.

It is important to offer individuals who take their first steps on an initiatory path a dedicated space, always the same, and a time of mystery, always the same. Every month, or every week, people come together in the same place, at the same time, in the world but protected from the world. The importance of respecting the dates of the schedule of meetings in Freemasonry, Martinism, Pythagoreanism, and Rosicrucianism is essential. The participants know that at a pre-arranged time, in a pre-arranged place, a particular setting is designated for them so that they use it for the foundation of their very existence. We can never stress enough the disastrous consequences of missed schedules, changes, postponements, or delays that contribute to the loss of the energies that are invited to gather in a lodge. In inner orders, any guest who arrives a single minute late is definitively dismissed. The practices contribute to a naturally harmonious and efficient setting of times and spaces. The more advanced the practice, the more the time is organized with fluidity around the practitioner. Synchronicity becomes a constant.

We are well aware that this time and this space are symbolic or of energetic nature but it is necessary to represent them materially so that the seeker can easily find his spatial and temporal landmarks. Later, much later, all time will be sacred, all place will be the place of mystery since the subject will have verified by experience that it is both the temple and the way.

Until the process of symbolization is actually completed—so that the subject carries the temple within him, and the temple is manifested by him, at every moment—walls and clocks remain necessary. This process of symbolization begins at an early age but does not end because we are adults. It is precisely in the lodge that this process will continue until the crossing of the individual from the phenomenal zone into the noumenal zone, from the noise of the world into the silence of Being. Then, the combination of glances will suffice to consecrate the space, a single sound, a single gesture, or better, synchronization of the breaths, will enable the conditioned profane to have time to unlock free access to the real.

As long as the lodge welcomes individuals whose needs solicit the exoteric function, that is to say, who need to be reconciled with themselves, with the environment and the world, to be in therapy in the Greek sense of the term, this containing space will be almost indispensable so that they can treat the complexities of their own particular set of problems. Once these things are played out, when they begin to leave the horizontality of the human experience to approach the verticality of Being, the formal moment, the formal space, and the formal time have less importance. We can open a sacred time with a snap of our fingers and close it with a click of the tongue. But if we propose this type of work prematurely, it can be destructive for the person because it may perhaps reproduce elements of his problem set in a space and time that are not contained. His personality can collapse. The reinforcing of the lodge and the ritual is necessary for a long time except in a few exceptional cases.

Circumstances sometimes require speeding up the disidentification. In wartime, some lodges gathered around a table. The sacred space was circumscribed at the table. The sacred time was the appropriate time. In times of conflict, the cultural and historical context are such that there is a particular tension, so this sacred space and time are created with and by the dimensions of risk.

Except for these extreme periods, the regularity of the initiatory time, the constant of the sacred space, will help the individual to register and structure within his own interiority. Later, it will be necessary to do the opposite work: a destructuring, or rather a deconstruction. The deconstruction of the person and his disintegration are only possible when the alliance with the Self is impossible to untie. The relationship with the Self must first be rooted.

Rules and knowledge

In a given setting, a sacred time and a consecrated space, knowledge and rules will be put into place.

What are these rules, that are simple and rarely respected? They are confidentiality, respect, and unconditionality.

- Confidentiality is different from secrecy. There is indeed an initiatory secret, or rather secrets. It is secret only because it touches the unspeakable and only the experience of ineffable reality can grasp its nature. Poetry in twilight language may hope, perhaps, to give a sense of it. Confidentiality is the consideration of the anonymity and the discretion of the brothers and sisters from their profane associates, who in no case should suffer from their commitment to the quest. Confidentiality is also the understanding that in the lodge we are in confidence. We deal with what is most intimate in the human experience, the life of the spirit. The individual can put within the lodge the aspects of the psyche that he cannot present outside this space and out of that time. Hence the importance of the lodge.
- Respect is first of all respect for oneself,[17] of one's own integrity, of one's own nobility of heart from which follows naturally the respect of the other, recognized as another self. It is not a question of morality, of respect for forms, but of respect for what remains, for the unconditioned. Indeed, we know the value of disrespect on the ways of liberation, disrespect of the fixed forms, the lies, the mediocrity, the baseness, the narrow-mindedness, ultimately, of the stupidity.

---

17 To think that a person can owe us something is a lack of respect for oneself.

- Unconditionality cannot be programmed. It is born from diligence in the practices and the increased consciousness which follows from it.

On the other hand, there are a certain number of traditional wisdoms that will be communicated and put to the test. This transmission, this implementation and this verification of the principles will be made in the lodge, at first, then outside the enclosure of the lodge.

The Companionage

The Companionage can be considered from three angles, that of the referent, that of the community, and that of the nomadic alternative.

- We have already pointed out the importance of the referent. It may be the sponsor, an elder sister or brother, a lodge instructor who has taken or accepted, depending on the circumstances, the responsibility of presenting and accompanying the recipient who has become a new initiate. His first quality will be listening, the second, observation. It is by listening and observing the subject that he will be able to evaluate to what extent the subject integrates the proposed settings, makes a creative alliance, understands the meaning of the initiatory work, and enters the initiatory process. He will note carefully whether the subject's needs have been identified and are likely to be met in the proposed work and settings. He will verify that the subject is congruent, that is to say that his thought, word, and action are integrated and harmoniously aligned. He will verify that the inevitable pretense in the early days is transformed into a sort of initiatory false-self. The gestures, the conventions, the ritual, the particular vocabulary, and the decorations are first practiced by mimicry and senselessly. If the meaning does not come to light, and it is only by practice that it will register in the consciousness, the subject will crystallize a semblance which will also be a pseudo-Being, an obstacle to the experience of Being.

- The community that represents the lodge is certainly a community of heart—brotherhood should animate all present—but it is especially a community of initiatory weapons. Each is a mirror of the other. The adventure requires that weapons are forged patiently by the practices. These weapons are called vigilance, attention, the objective state, presence, sharpness of the mind, behavioral flexibility, and internal verticality. Each develops some skills in a favored way and acquires others with difficulty. Mutual enrichment through the exchange of skills is the very justification of the lodge community. If this dynamic is not internal to the community, the mode of initiation lineage is preferable in every respect because it does not have all the disadvantages of group life. This mutuality will be orchestrated (and that is the correct term), by the venerable of the lodge in Freemasonry or by the initiator in non-Masonic currents. This dimension of the connection is fundamental, and here we find our initial paradox: it is the weaving of the connections between people of adventure, without dependence, that will promote the experience of the interval, of the middle chamber, the sudden descent into emptiness that constitutes the authentic encounter with Being. Indeed, there can be no interval without continuity. An interval is impossible to spot in a discontinuous and chaotic field. All holes in consciousness are not access to the real, some on the contrary are of a pathological nature. If there is a possible direct path from disorder to awakening, it is not in the setting of a lodge that it can be explored. It requires other conditions that cannot be brought together in the context of Masonic structures.

In the container that the community represents, the quester will learn to play with the connections, to make and undo the forms without disruption or disrupting the energy in presence. He will realize that what he believes to be outside is inside and that henceforth, wherever he is, the community, the lodge, the order, and the world remain in him. He is his own world, his own creation.

Once this internal source is accessed, the nomadic alternative, true companionage, can be offered.

- The nomadic alternative does not lie in the possibility of "visiting" lodges of the same obedience or "friendly" obediences, which imply the existence of "enemy" obediences. The nomadic alternative, which is a necessary step in the initiatory process, consists of a real journey into closed or different traditions. In the same way that a person who learns a foreign language, then two, then three, actually learns to learn foreign languages, a quester who explores and practices a tradition until exhaustion, then a second and a third, experiences the absolute structure that lies behind the traditions. Some would speak of the "Tradition of Traditions." Therefore, wherever he is, in whatever tradition he is, he is in his home. Whatever the ritual, he grasps the essence, whatever the exercise, he grasps the principle. It is only from this moment, when the quester is freed from the forms imposed by culture, history, and people, that we can truly speak of initiation. Few lodges, Masonic or otherwise, organize this type of work for fear of "losing" a member, or even more so from the unconscious fear of what is foreign. It is up to the initiator, the referent, and the community to prepare each one for this journey, to leave the lodge, and to judge the moment of departure. Too soon, the poorly trained traveler can fall from one identification to another, from one belief to another instead of going beyond the world of beliefs. Too late, the subject, too cramped in the setting of the lodge or the order, will attack the setting or wither.

5 The Initiatory Process

> "Yes, good people, it is I who order you to burn, on a shovel reddened in the fire and with a little yellow sugar, the duck of doubt with vermouth lips, which, in a melancholy struggle between good and evil, spills tears that do not come from the heart and creates everywhere, without a pump, a universal void. This is the best you can do."
>
> ISIDORE DUCASSE—Comte de Lautréamont. *Poems I.*

The investment of initiatory work

The initiatory work has two main parts that will differ according to the order, the rite, the lodge, and the individual but will have the same perspective: awakening. An initiatory path that would not be considered as a way of awakening is without the slightest interest. These two components consist of a corpus and practices.

- The corpus is composed of a set of fundamental texts particular to the current, the order, and the lodge in which they are inscribed, but also of a literary and artistic corpus without which the initiate cannot access a true traditional culture. How to avoid, for the West, Rabelais, Cervantes and Dante? More recently, how to avoid Lautréamont? It is heartbreaking that the lodges are filled with uneducated and ignorant people who are not readers. The whole dimension that can be integrated among the Companions by the operative work of the hands and the extension of the spirit will be found in speculative literature, if the reader is able to distinguish the background of the literature that poses the same question as science, philosophy, and initiation: "Why is there something rather than nothing?" If the apprentice can neither read nor write, it is because he has yet to learn to read and to think. Until then, he has only scribbled and "opined." But thought is born of silence, not of mental agitation.

The traditional corpus, which is hermetic in most cases, therefore deserves to be inserted into a larger literary and artistic ensemble. The discerning researcher will discover that nothing that is stated in traditional corpora is ignored in literature and art. All arcana are found in poetry, painting, sculpture, and music; indeed, there are many artists and writers who have the sense of Being. Many are confronted with the crucial issue of death.

- The practices of an order with a truly initiatory orientation all concur in conquering the zone of silence, silencing internal dialogue and reactive emotions, to bathe in this infinite interval in which Being, our own nature, is encountered. While many exercises can be offered, they are in fact the different and variegated skins of one and the same exercise which is set out in four or five modalities. The multiplication of exercises is a way of satisfying the mind and fighting against boredom or renunciation. This multiplication is often ineffective because only one who is aware that he is always practicing, in all circumstances, the same exercise, that of consciousness and the movement of energy, is progressing. He will understand the principles rather than the forms. What is true for the martial arts is true for the other initiatory arts.

The instructor knows that behind one exercise is always another exercise. It is up to him to determine what is the appropriate exercise, in what form, with what dosage, what frequency, taking into account the psycho-physical structure of the practitioner.

The quality of the investment in the initiatory work obviously determines its efficiency and the initiate's progress.

There is of course, in any external structure, a significant proportion of subjects who do not invest in the work. These are clearly undesirable. There are those who invest only in the corpus, and this is a defense mechanism of the "person" against the coming of Being in itself. These seekers, often brilliant, who are likely to have good "careers" in the orders, can be encouraged to restore a balance between study and practice, which is not without difficulty. There are those who, having no taste for study and reading, will stick to practices. Study can then be replaced by craftwork or going into nature.

We have observed four modes of investment in initiatory work: specific investment, personal expression, striving to perform, and explicit communication. According to the individuals, according to the phases of the initiatory process, according to the personal, family, professional and traditional contexts, these four modes will be more or less predominant.

The balance will require that the commitment be first specific, i.e., that the subject practices without question, scrupulously respecting the form, and even without seeking results, until the first effects in the consciousness appear. Then the desired state is put in place, for example, an increased consciousness. The exercise hidden behind the formal exercise can then clearly be identified, in principle, by the subject. An explicit communication about the subject's experience can subsequently be useful and necessary. Prior to that, it would have been premature, since the mind could artificially create the supposed effect. Let us remember that experience is always superior to the idea and that only that which is lived, tested, and verified in and by the body and mind of the subject contributes to the quest. The rest, everything else, is an obstacle.

When the principle is approached, the practitioner will transform the form of the exercise. His personal expression will change the configuration without altering the principle. We can speak of initiatory art and this is a preparation for the realization of initiatory *performances,* just as there are artistic *performances.* If the principle is altered by personal expression, that is a sign that it has not been identified.

In certain phases, the practitioner can be in the performance, in "holding fast,"[18] maintaining the posture. There is always a risk that this performance will be transformed into competition with one's peers or even oneself, which would be particularly harmful. These periods of over-effort have their purpose, certainly to push back the limits, but especially through an enantiodromic effect[19] to provoke a letting go, an interval in the flow of the mental representation, and an access to the real.

Explicit communication about the practice succeeds through parsimony. Naming what is anchored by experience is effective. Naming what is not experienced strengthens the net of illusions. In his relation to language, the researcher must take into account the elliptic and metaphorical dimension of language. The twilight language or silence of an instructor is explained by his resolve not to freeze a process. Any nominalization fixes the process. The word "love" freezes the process "love." A nominalization is only

---

18 "Holding fast is true prayer," according to Louis-Claude de Saint-Martin.

19 Brutal passage from one extreme to the other, for example from love to hate.

effective if the experience it will designate is powerful and can be reactivated at will. The initiatory process takes place before putting oneself into words.

The three phases of the initiatory process

We can identify three phases in the initiatory process, corresponding to three trials.

- The first phase is the mastery of the higher symbolic function. The implementation of this function, normally installed in early childhood, will be resumed, or more exactly reoriented progressively, in terms of archetypes. Corpus, practices, and instructions install in the subject a sophisticated symbolic toolkit made from tools of representation specific to the initiatory current in which the order is inscribed. These tools directly mobilize the great archetypal energies without going through language. They constitute an alphabet and a geometry of energies. Sounds, images, and abstractions are the most common forms. A symbol is efficient if it spontaneously triggers the state of consciousness, or the corresponding energy process, by a kind of synesthesia. Neither the hexagram nor the pentagram are present in the lodge for a dissertation, but for the mobilization of energies and the orientation of an increased consciousness.

    To connect the symbols present in the temple to the practices is the responsibility not only of the master and the officers of the lodge but of everyone who enters the temple, according to his own experience.

    This new appropriation of the symbolic function will be a very useful tool for the subject who will approach the question behind all questions, the original fear behind all other fears. This question is that of his own death. This fear is a primitive fear, felt before even giving it a form. There is, from the first stammerings of life in this body, which is also the body of death and the body of realization, the feeling of a threat. The nature of this threat determines in part the initiatory process in its first phase.

If there is a threat to the identity of the subject, to the "who am I?" or the axis of temporality, the process will take the symbolic form of a path of immortality, an immortality to endure. It will be a magical, progressive way (since there is time). This path is qualified by the expression: "In the beginning was the word," and can be described by the following nominalizations: *Isolate* and *Nominate* to leave the implicit world—*Oppose* and *Differentiate* to create duality—*Identify, Identify with, Invoke, Symbolize* to establish oneself in the explicit world—*Co-create* and *Re-unite* to go beyond duality and return, conscious, to the implicit world...

If there is a threat to the singularity of the subject, to the "What is my place?" or the axis of spatiality, the process will take the symbolic form of a quest for eternity, or interiority. It will be a direct way (since there is no time). This path applies to the expression dear to Goethe: "In the beginning was the deed," and can be described by the process *Isolate, Act,* and *Name* to leave the implicit world—*Transform* and *Imagine* to create duality—*Remember* and *Symbolize* to establish oneself in the explicit world—*Co-create* and *Re-unite* to go beyond duality and return, conscious, to the implicit world...

- If these two processes are followed by ellipses, it is because both of them lead to the entry into Silence. This is the second phase of the initiatory process, the most important phase, the obligatory phase, which can be qualified by the expression "Before the beginning, there is Silence."

It is in the zone of silence, the Middle Chamber of the Freemasons, the field of non-representation in which the Real sings, that the initiate can operate by theurgy and by alchemy, just as by the *Art of Doing Nothing*. It is therefore well after, and not before, access to silence and the void, well within the void, in the very dimension of silence, that the adept operates. Any theurgy, any alchemy, internal or external, implemented in the chaos and noise of the "person," is not only vain but probably toxic because it densifies and crystallizes the fears and anxieties of the mind. A good synonym for "mind" is the word "trouble." Operating in a troubled zone can only generate monstrosities or, at the least, ridicule. That is why Meister Eckhart says, "All the works that man does outside the Kingdom of God are dead works, but those he does in the Kingdom of God are living works."

We cannot dwell enough on the fact, which has been incessantly demonstrated, that no initiation is accessible apart from silence. It is in the silence and in the void that the real ways are born, it is there that they begin, it is there that they unfold, it is there that they finish, in a perfect simultaneity.

The second trial is thus the void-silence itself.

- The third phase, of which nothing can be said, is the realization of being, or of Being—the capital letter is there for a reason. This is not a phase in which something is to be done, or in which something is to be obtained, it is on the contrary a phase characterized by the absence of doing and having, by the absence of the "person." It is a phase in which the Being emerges, occupying the place left unoccupied by the "person" in the field of consciousness. The process has mutated into a non-process.

To recap: The first phase is a phase of reconciliation, of rapprochement with the axis of oneself which is also the axis of the world, of the comprehension that reality and dream are of the same nature and, consequently, that the Real is other. The second phase is a phase of disidentification with the "person" and the world. The third phase is a dive into the Real. Meister Eckhart, again, is explicit: "And when the soul is made luminescent and discovers the endless circle, then it rushes to the center."

In a certain way, in other words, in the first phase we end the egoic process, we push the construction of the self into these last entrenchments, where it is nothing more than limits. In the second, we let the self dissolve into silence and emptiness. In the third, Being reigns.

The practices concern the person and are a call to Being. But once the mask has fallen, the process requires no intervention and unfolds naturally. It is the person who is against nature. Being is our original and ultimate nature.

6 Assessment of the Initiatory Process

> "One can only judge the beauty of life by that of death. [...] One can only judge the beauty of death by that of life."
>
> ISIDORE DUCASSE—Comte de Lautréamont. *Poems II.*

The triangle: referent-initiator-Self

On several occasions we have used the concept of the referent without really defining it. We also indicated that the setting of the individual project solicited three types of alliances: an alliance with a referent, an alliance with the initiator or with the Master of the lodge, and an alliance with the Self. We must now try to identify the technical issue of the triangle referent-initiator-Self.

The word referent causes us to think in general of the sponsor in Freemasonry but it can be another initiate altogether, who is at the same time the friend, the confidant, and the elder brother with regard to the quest in which the recipient is engaged. He accompanies him at his side, not to sweep the difficulties out from under his feet, but to prevent him from falling into ruts from which he cannot extricate himself. The referent respects the autonomy of the subject. He does not do the work for him. He indicates the interest of certain paths or certain layovers. At times he praises idleness and at times he invites overexertion.

The initiator, in Freemasonry the Venerable Master most often, always represents the East, the central axis, and the Real. He should be an immutable and illuminating reference point in the life of the lodge, but this of course raises the question of the quality of the training and the work of the lodges. His action is of a different nature from that of the referent. While the referent acts at the periphery of human experience, in the conditioned, the initiator always recalls the unconditionality of the quest, the immutable, that which remains. He does not accompany on the way, but he lights the way.

The referent and the initiator only represent the Self in the world of the explicit. The true referent is the Self, the Being in oneself. While waiting for this Self to emerge in the field of consciousness, the referent and the initiator, in their own modality, will not cease to lead the initiate to the experience of the Self.

Referent, initiator and Self use the same mirror effect. The referent refers to the initiate a benevolent image of himself, whilst the initiator conveys to him a future image of himself, that of the accomplished initiate, the goal to reach, the reason for his entry onto the path of the initiation. The distance between the two causes the movement. Self refers to consciousness the undistorted image of human reality to better dissolve all images, all reflections, and all representations. This mirror of consciousness, polished by the practices, has for its subject emotion and not intellect. The emotional mirror is a formidable efficiency. The passage from a conditioned emotion to a free emotion, purely energetic and conscious as such in itself, makes it possible to pose the grammatically incorrect question: Who am I, the reality, in the presence of... my fear, my hate, my love, my joy, my guilt?

The initiator assures and embodies the transmission, even if the transmission is in fact only a decoy intended to reinforce the initiatory process, while the referent assists in picking the fruits of the transmission. The true initiator is the Self, the only fruit is the Self and the Being in oneself.

The quality of the mediation between the referent, the initiator, and the initiate will be one of the determinants of the autonomy of the initiate. We could probably identify various degrees of autonomy corresponding to different stages of the mirror process. It suffices to understand that when the constraints of the person are released, and as the pathological need to tell stories to build up his "personal legend" is erased, the initiate accesses his own reality and it is his reality itself that generates and develops the initiatory process.

Assessment and self-assessment

There is therefore a need for an assessment. What is assessed is not the subject of course, but the process.

Assessing a subject is inadmissible. No one can judge. It is necessary to end the pretense of knowing what right is. We measure the stupidity of Masonic tribunals while struggling to construct proper justice in the heart of the city.

To judge the person is to put her in resistance, to jeopardize the process of detachment from the "mask" of presuppositions, prejudices, beliefs, and other conditioning. How do we drop the masks so that Being springs forth, if the whole person, feeling threatened, refuses to enter the process of initiation, without this covenant with the Self? The person must be in a sufficiently contained and reassuring environment to accept being stared at.

Assessing a process is not only possible but desirable even if we remain aware that this assessment is relative and contextual. The assessment will be based on the exchange of views: the close view of the referent, the more distant view of the initiator, the intimate view of the initiate. This ability to self-assess the initiatory process by the initiate, initially halting, will develop through practice to become fully functional and instinctive.

The best quality of information for any assessment is behavioral. No one can deceive an informed gaze because the body always delivers, even subtly, the incongruence or the congruence of the person. Every belief is behavioral. Every belief generates behaviors. Careful observation of behavior helps to distinguish the unconscious beliefs that animate the person.

Emotional information will be the second field of assessment. The ability to let emotions live in the field of consciousness, allowing them to develop as energies in motion, without intervening, without re-acting, is an excellent barometer of Self-remembering.

Finally, the intellectual matter, the understanding of what is there, will be the most difficult to take into account. Indeed, the mind can display a very brilliant intellectual understanding of the initiatory path and the philosophies of enlightenment, as a powerful mechanism of self-defense.

While speech can be misleading, especially for oneself, we cannot fake our ability of silence or emptiness, of our relationship to time, of our energy density... which reflect the quality of our relationship to Being or to the Real.

The special moments when, together, the initiator, the referent, and the initiate examine with serenity the current process constitute the formation of the initiatory subject. The initiate is truly the only subject of the initiatory process. Initiation consists in passing from an object conditioned by its environment to a subject free from all conditioning.

7 The Theory of "Three Persons" in the Initiatory Process

> "Man knows that his reign has no end and that the universe has a beginning. The universe knows nothing: it is, at most, a thinking reed."
>
> ISIDORE DUCASSE—Comte de Lautréamont. *Poems II.*

THE MODEL PRESENTED BELOW, like any model, does not describe the reality, but allows us to think of the reality of the initiatory process. This model is not a truth but a working tool that suits some things and is not suitable for others.

The secular person and the sacred person

Initiation introduces a sacred enclosure. There is an inside, sacred, and an outside, profane. They are radically different models of the world, different codes for outside and inside, different languages, different clothes, and different visual and sensory environments. This is reflected in the classic opposition between modernity and tradition, between education and initiation.

This artificial distinction is pedagogical. Initiation creates a cleavage in the person. There is the profane person, the "old man," old but still alive, and the sacred person, the "new man," new but not yet freed and autonomous.

The profane person is made of the tight weaving of the familial, cultural, professional, and other conditionings inscribed since the conception of the individual, but also of the packaging transmitted by heredity.

The sacred person builds himself up on the basis of the new conditioning caused by the work in the lodge, the traditional studies, and the individual practices. All experience installs conditioning, the components of which are called criteria, values, beliefs, strategies, and processes. It is not possible to live in an unconditioned way. It is possible to get rid of conditioning by creating new conditioning that will allow such freedom. To break free, it is sometimes appropriate to use a thorn to remove thorns already marked in the flesh.

This cleavage in the person is technically interesting because it creates an interval between the two persons, a crack in the personal legend that the practices will enlarge into a breach then into a wide door giving access to Being. That is why, at first, this artificial opposition between the profane and the sacred is necessary. It is a technique, not an ideology. We will observe that the sacred person does not have the same behaviors as the profane person, that the concern for ethics and fraternity present in the sacred precinct tends to fade in the profane world.

Cleavage must be generated starting with the first initiation. If the passage beneath the blindfold is efficient, it must leave a slight crack in the continuity of the person, in his model of the world. Initiation will merely turn this slight crack into a fissure. The deeper the fissure is, deep before it is widened, the deeper it descends into the depths of the psyche, and the more it allows the radiance of the light of Being.

The farther the distance is between the profane person and the sacred person, the easier it is for psychic mobility. The more the harmonious integration of the personality is facilitated, the more the cleavage is effective.

If the impact of the profane person remains far beyond the influence of the sacred person, the formal setting is maintained at all costs and there is a risk of the profane intruding into the sacred.

If the impact of the sacred person is greater than the normal radiance of the profane person, the risk of irruption of the profane into the sacred is zero.

The witness, third person

The initiatory cleavage of the person cannot continue in the absence of adequate practices. In most Western initiations, we can consider that a ceremony even conducted without consciousness, in a stereotypical manner, produces the effect of cleavage. But in most initiatory orders, the proposed exercises, when they exist, are spiritualistic rather than initiatory. They nourish the beliefs of the sacred person rather than leading to self-remembering and silence. Also, the cleavage either becomes pathological if the initiated person has a poorly integrated personality, or disappears slowly and surely, the person unifying his two parts to regain his initial integrity.

To maintain the cleavage a third person, a third term, will therefore be introduced by self-remembering practices and self-presence. This is the witness. The witness is no more real than the profane person and the sacred person. It is also born of a cleavage of the person and more precisely of the observation of the game between the profane person and the sacred person. It will be the "lucid part" whose mission will be to become more and more aware of what is happening in the field of human experience.

Cleavage in three parts has several advantages. It maintains open access to Being, until Being is so installed in the field of consciousness that the person is no more than an accessory, one element among others of the environment.

It is a factor of balance of the personality. Experience shows that if the two-part cleavage can lead to imbalance and haze, the three-part cleavage stabilizes the person around a new verticality experienced in the body, also by a distant, lucid, and humorous view, interpreting and affecting our experiences.

This last point is important because it suggests that giving the initiation without giving the means for initiation amounts to inoculating against a virus when one does not know whether it will produce disastrous effects if the person is not sufficiently immune.

The posture of the third person

This posture, this view of the witness will permit awareness of certain fundamentals:

The conditioned person does not have access to the Real.

The common human does not live in the Real but in its representation. This representation is primarily sensory. It is the deep structure of human experience. The human being is incapable of objectivity. Its main quality is its own subjectivity, the source of its creativity.

Language constructs a secondary representation of the Real. It is the surface structure of human experience, the spoken and thought structure. The elliptical character of language made of generalizations, omissions, and distortions distances us even more from the Real than does the sensory.

Experience is superior to the idea. Our beliefs, our presuppositions, our criteria, and our values, for the most part unconscious, are born from our experiences, direct or vicarious.

The potent power-territory-reproduction triangle underlies all our actions, words, and thoughts. Reproduction means not only sexual reproduction[20] but the reproduction of *myself*, the person, in the same way. This triangle is that of the survivor. Without it, the human species would have long since disappeared, hence its power. It is the energies of this triangle that will be the material of the initiatory process. Initiation consists in orienting these primitive energies in the verticality of Being rather than letting them extend into the temporal and spatial horizontality of human experience.

The initiatory work consists in identifying these archaic forces, taming them, orienting them, and crowning them with Being. Initiation is not for the person.

The initiatory work triggers the process but does not control it. No exercise allows you to switch to the Real. The exercises lead almost "mechanically" to silence and emptiness. On the other hand, the experience of Being and the fullness of emptiness is not a matter of technique.

The culmination of the process

The practices will lead to a permanence of the witness, to an exit of identifications and to a state that is often called the objective state, which however does not correspond to the conscious experience of the Real indicated by the word "awakening," not yet. In the objective state, the game of the person is recognized for what it is, a masquerade that veils the Real by successive superimpositions. The objective state is a form of increased awareness of what is there, of forms and especially the energy of forms, that in which we have life, movement, and being.

---

20 One of the functions of religion is the control of women and therefore of reproduction, which is why women's freedom has always frightened the great monotheistic patriarchal religions, including totalitarian politics of the right or left that are structured and oriented like religions.

With the permanence of the witness, the meeting and the reduction of the profane person and the sacred person will be a simple formality. The permanence of the witness makes it possible to go beyond the columns, beyond the pairs of opposites. There is no more interior and exterior, dream and reality, profane and sacred. The person will float in the scenery as one element among others unrelated to Being in itself. It disappears completely only with physical death, only the fixation is erased. It is dying before you die. "I" is no longer identified with the person, just "I am."

The witness himself will disappear to give place, the whole place, to Being.

We can also observe an absorption of the profane person by the sacred person, a sacralisation, under the gaze of the witness, before the detachment of the person.

When the process of sacralisation is faster than the process of disidentification to the person, we will speak of the magic way. When, conversely, the process of disidentification is faster than the process of sacralisation, it will be a direct way.

Perhaps it is necessary to insist on the fact that we are in the presence of a natural process, that is simply a question of removing the superimpositions which stifle the original Being, of returning from the multiple to the one. Initiation is always a simplification.

For those who find the alchemical metaphor more meaningful, we could consider the person as the first matter. The profane person would then be a Mercury, the sacred person a Sulphur, and the witness a Salt. Being would be the Red Stone. This only applies as a metaphor.

We are aware that this model of the initiatory process does not flatter the person. It leaves no room for a spirituality which is only one activity of the person among others. On the other hand, it poses some of the inevitable and fundamental "data" of the ways of awakening.

8 Dysfunctions in the Initiatory Process

"Suffering is weakness, when one can help oneself and do something better."
ISIDORE DUCASSE—Comte de Lautréamont. *Poems I.*

THE OBSERVATION MUST BE MADE that most so-called initiatory orders are inoperative. The model outlined above can help us identify the types of dysfunctions most frequently encountered in traditional Masonic structures. Recall that talking about "dysfunction" implies, despite everything, a function.

Dysfunctions in the group or obedience

Most of the obediences and traditional orders have a hard time escaping the action of the "Luciferian" (and not "diabolical") triangle of power-territory-reproduction. Internal struggles, competitions between organizations, the "professionalization" and "commodification" of initiation are commonplace. They reflect the radical break with traditional rules and principles and the lack of initiatory work by the leaders of these organizations more concerned with their careers than with their awakening.

There is no reason to blame them for this personal inclination. It is always difficult to really enter the initiatory process, to escape one's conditioning. A powerful "will" is needed to fertilize the Being in the soil hidden behind the person. However, we can regret the rapid deterioration of viable traditional structures under the impact of numbers and multiplication. This degradation does not facilitate the emergence of initiatory processes. It doesn't stop it, either.

Admittedly, the institutional setting is not guaranteed (that of the lodge is threatened), but the process being natural and original, it can be enough of an encounter to trigger it. The companionage may be faulty if the setting of the lodge is affected, but the internal reference and the influence of the Self may be sufficient for a path to emerge.

Those who abandon the way and the initiatory work under the pretext of a disappointment within the lodge, rite, or obedience, are simply not ready for initiation. On the contrary, there are all those who turn this disappointment into strength. They realize that it is not the traditional forms, the human structures, so fallible, that they must hunt down, but the initiatory, informal, and unconditioned paths of the human.

We can consider this almost general degradation as inherent in the Kali Yuga, the reign of the caste of merchants. A careful observation of the life of the obediences shows that a shopkeeper state of mind dominates there, between barter, sale, and slavery. This deleterious state is perhaps more a given than a dysfunction. To consider it as such seems to be an excellent presupposition because, rather than dwelling on dysfunctions, it compels us to take this given as a simple element of the profane environment.

To avoid cascading repercussions within a traditional order, some structures have chosen partitioning or a decentralized organization.

The strict partitioning between groups or the partitioning between ranks within them can reduce the risks of dysfunctions specific to the life of the groups. It can be technically justified.

Some operative practices require a minimum of isolation and relative silence. Contacts within the order with unqualified members can be difficult. The partitioning must be either clearly explained or totally invisible so as not to create, by simple incomprehension, feelings of rejection, dissensions, and tensions in the organization.

Decentralized organizations such as networks of free initiators simplify procedures and reduce the risk of spreading crises but can promote wilting or impoverishment.

Inviting the recipient, from the beginning of the work, to lucidity, to concentrate on the way and not on the traditional form, seems more necessary than ever. There is no point in entertaining illusions about initiatory orders that ultimately only render service. Let's not forget that we are dealing with human groups. We will further reduce dysfunctions by a practice that precisely restricts the role of the conditioned human, rather than by an organizational mode.

Dysfunctions in one or the other person

We saw in the previous chapter that initiation establishes a sacred person and a profane person and a third term called the witness. This new provisional structuring of the ego, favorable to the implementation of the initiatory process, can be complicated.

Dysfunctions in the profane person

Issues within the profane person can be revealed by initiation. If these issues are proven disorders, they are relevant to psychotherapy and we can then speak of an error of indication and orientation. This person should not have been accepted into a traditional lodge and must be directed to psychotherapeutic currents under the label of personal development, or in the case of a sufficiently deep relationship with the person, invited directly to consult a doctor or psychotherapist.

If the disorder is not proven but the person is on the way to a disorder, can the lodge take the risk to continue the process? This question will have to be assessed on a case-by-case basis. It is not the task of an initiatory order to conduct therapeutic work—it must be done outside. Note in passing the total incompatibility between the initiatory approach and psychoanalytic cure. It is up to the referent, the initiator, and possibly the most experienced members of the lodge, in full agreement with the subject, to decide whether the subject can conduct a therapeutic approach and an initiatory approach and in what ways. In this case, the function of the Hospitaller brother deserves to be rethought. It could take on a different scale than the one that is commonly allowed.

Irruption of the profane person in the sacred person

It is frequent, once the shock and surprise of the initiation is removed and once the effect of the rupture with the profane is blurred, that the border between the profane and the sacred becomes permeable. Profane behaviors can then emerge in the field of the sacred and disrupt the life of the lodge. For example, there can be a need to justify oneself or a tendency to long superficial discussions or oratorical jousting.

An adjustment or reinforcement of the practices of division of the consciousness, which favor self-remembering, the presence to oneself, a benevolent interview using the process of the mirror, will be sufficient in most cases to restore the strict setting of the initiatory work. This is often just a slip-up.

Invasion of the sacred person by the profane person

In this case, profane concerns gradually resume possession of the field of consciousness.

This is the most common case in Masonic obediences. The

setting of the lodge is not guaranteed by the Venerable Master of the lodge. The border between sacred and profane is vague or shifting. For example, the work deals with non-traditional issues or traditional issues in a psychological fashion. The time of the works has not been sacralized, the sacred space has not been preserved. It is not uncommon to see an entire lodge profaned. There is no more distinction between the profane and the sacred because everything is profane behind a scarcely maintained facade of the sacred. Note that the formal setting of the lodge can be flexible if the symbolic frame is strong. But it will probably be necessary, through prescriptions of tasks, to reformulate the setting for individuals with weak symbolic investment until they fully master the symbolic function.

The sincerity of most is not in question. Sincerity, desire for initiation, and commitment are most often present initially. The initiatory path is open but it is the absence of an answer in terms of practices and traditional teachings that first allows the primary access to Being to be closed under a layer of sediments (the fallout of the conditioned superimpositions onto Being that the initiation had lifted) and then that the sacred person, badly nourished, poorly protected, that is to say badly manhandled, withdraws. The absence of an initiatory practice sooner or later leads to the trivialization of the sacred and it is a prelude to its invasion by the profane because the profane conditionings are particularly stubborn and inclined to expand and strengthen.

If the practice does not institute the third person who will witness this contest between the profane person and the sacred person, the initiatory process does not start. The position of witness reinforces the initiation and development process of the sacred person because, in the position of witness, the initiate can evaluate the process, adjust it, and use profane tendencies as a matter of initiatory work.

Cannibalization of the profane person by the sacred person

It is possible, outside the installation of the witness, that we observe a cannibalization of the profane person by the sacred person. It is often a violent experience that causes a visible change of personality, very quickly, even immediately after an initiation or reception. Ordinarily, the candidate for initiation who undergoes this type of experience presents an exacerbated need for recognition and belonging.

The sacred person literally "devours" the profane person. The word is appropriate as the process is expeditious. Without a witness, he becomes a new profane person because the sacred is determined only in opposition to the profane. However, he will have integrated a model of the spiritualistic or religious world in a radical way. Fanatics show this type of dysfunction.

It will be extremely difficult to conduct this category of people, who substitute a simulacrum of the sacred for the sacred inherent in nature, toward a real initiation.

These dysfunctions are easily identifiable. We notice that they develop in a toxic way only in the absence of the witness.

It is the practices that contribute to the remembering of oneself, to the entry into silence, to the experience of emptiness that constitutes the key to the initiatory process. They are at the same time the true setting, independent of human culture and organization, a sacred enclosure without walls, and yet a container and a path in its own right.

Dysfunctions of the witness

An intensive practice of self-remembering by the division of consciousness[21] is often accompanied in its beginnings by a certain tension around the constitution of the witness.

From the new effort required of the individual to produce the witness, a tension is born that can be felt throughout the body. After a few weeks, the fluidity of movement returns with the integration of the witness's posture almost effortlessly. However, in some cases, the tension is fixed, and crystallizes into trouble. The profane person takes on the witness in order to protect himself from his own annihilation. This reversal is manifested by a coldness and a stiffness both physical and psychic, a distance from the human experience lived in a too dissociated way, a mistrust vis-à-vis the emotional sphere, and an identification with the dis-identification.

There is frequently confusion about control of the emotions. It is not the emotion itself that should be eradicated but the reaction to emotion. We usually live so little in our emotions that we confuse them with our reactions to emotion. Emotion is an energetic movement that springs from a stimulus, develops, reaches a peak, then decreases in intensity and eventually fades. In the position of witness, we let the emotion live the whole of this deployment, without reacting, without interpreting, without making a personal narrative. Simply, "that" happens. In this case, the energy deployed remains available. However, emotion is usually grasped very early by the person who interprets it, comments on it, constrains it, tries to reduce it or, on the contrary, to intensify

---

21 The expression *division of consciousness* can be confusing. Exercises of this type tend to unify consciousness. By dividing the conscious attention between several senses, they aim at stopping the internal dialogue and give access to an increased perceptive awareness of "what is there." One can thus speak of *division of attention*.

it by the artifices of language, sometimes to repeat it indefinitely.

In the witness's posture, the emotion completes its entire journey before returning to its source without loss. We can taste all the flavor. Without emotions, the human being could not survive. Fear, in particular, is necessary for survival, but not the "white fear," the fear not of what happens but of what has happened and is no longer happening, of what could have happened or what could happen in the morbid activity of the person.

The witness remains effective if it remains close to the person, profane or sacred, if the person feels just under the witness's gaze, just below and not at a great distance.

The posture of the witness loses its strength and interest for our purpose if it is maintained with permanent effort. Association with the experience of the moment and dissociation, under the gaze, must alternate like a breath.

To overcome this type of dysfunction, practices of self-remembering, which may prove to be too desiccating, will be associated with practices of meditation on emptiness as in the practice of the letter **A**[22] or the practice of the five points of the heart.

---

22 Rémi Boyer, *Mask Cloak Silence: Martinism as a Way of Awakening* (Bayonne, NJ: Rose Circle, 2021), pp. 160–163.

9 Questions and Answers

> "One can be fair, if one is not human."
> ISIDORE DUCASSE—Comte de Lautréamont. *Poems II.*

THE QUESTIONS AND ANSWERS THAT FOLLOW come from the many seminars conducted by the author in Europe, especially in Masonic circles, on the theme of the practice of initiation.

What is the ultimate function of ritual? Is it essential?

The history of initiatory societies has shown that external or semi-internal initiatory orders without rituals are not viable. Only inner orders that have gone beyond work on forms can be freed from ritual because the ritual is replaced by the conscious movement of consciousness and energy. But there are many who, freed from the need for forms, continue to celebrate rites, without expecting anything, for beauty and joy.

The ritual has a sacralizing function. It is that which seals the sacred space and time. It also presents a container function by offering the person a space-time in which the encounter with Being can be approached.

On the other hand, it is necessary to distinguish within the ritual itself, the ceremonial rite.[23] The ceremonial allows the brothers and sisters gathered in the sacred enclosure to gradually prepare for silence and to escape from the troubled zone to enter the peaceful garden in which the rite will be operated. The ceremonial is always the support of self-remembering, a slow advance toward oneself, the unconditioned. And it is only in the shared silence, all internal dialogues extinguished, that the rite can be practiced. The ceremonial covers almost all the time of the ritual. The rite, as such, requires only two or three minutes of true silence, the time of the lighting of one, three, or seven torches and an invocation. The invocation is born of silence. The word springs from emptiness since it did not pre-exist. The operative invents, creates, and generates each word of the invocation in this very moment. A ritual is never the repetition of a past act, for each time it is a creation here and now. Every time is the very first time. Memory, another face of time, is erased for the non-time of the invocation.

How, technically, can we reach this level of invocational work?

By conscious breath. Therefore, in a simple and difficult way. Simple, because it's child's play. Difficult because the mind, which feeds on hypercomplexity and agitation, hates the simple. It gets bored as soon as we go into simplicity.

We know the importance of conscious breathing associated

---

23 Etymologically, the ritual, from the Latin *ritualis*, designates the elements written to lead the ceremonies, whereas the rite, Latin *ritus*, refers not only to all the ceremonies used in a religion or tradition but also the gesture or sequence of gestures prescribed by the liturgy. We consider here the rite as the operative element of the ritual, which inscribes in the verticality, on the axis, in the center, while the ceremonial leads to this verticality.

with the division of consciousness[24] for self-remembering and access to silence. We know less about its function in ritual. It is conscious breathing, both individual and collective, that produces the fire without which a ritual is only an amiable performance. How does one apply conscious breathing in the ceremonial to make the rite work? It is a question of inscribing the totality of the gestures, the words, and even the thoughts, which should be increasingly scarce, in the breath. The work starts well before the event. Ideally, the morning of the working, as soon as we get up, we should begin to divide the consciousness, to breathe consciously and to orient ourselves toward the evening work. Also be aware that our sisters and brothers are preparing in the same way. Be aware of the movement of beings who will join to share an experience of the sacred. If we orient all day toward the evening work, we will arrive at the lodge in an increased awareness and carrying a great energy even if our preparation is very imperfect.

In the temple, every movement, every word can be written in the waves of the breath. This means, for example, beginning each move, each utterance, at the beginning of the expiration, or the shifts in the interval between expiration and inspiration, and the words in the interval between inspiration and expiration. At first, there is always a little tension. With practice, we find fluidity and naturalness. It is an individual work. However, those who regularly approach the ritual in this way can verify that there is a natural and unconscious synchronization of the breaths of all at the approach of the rite: I do not believe that it is necessary to explain the power of this communion of the breaths that will bring the invocation to the summit of the rite.

---

24 For those interested in this technical aspect, read, among other things, "The Quadrant of Awakening" in *Mask Cloak Silence: Martinism as a Way of Awakening* by Rémi Boyer (Bayonne, NJ: Rose Circle, 2021), pp. 153–171.

The ceremonial may be replaced by a series of self-remembering exercises. It is interesting, on occasion, to replace the classic working with a "power." A "power" consists of a looping repetition of self-remembering exercises followed by ritual, self-remembering exercises and rituals. Each cycle sees the power of the rite intensify to an apogee that allows the experimenters to discover the true nature of the ritual practiced. An invocation is also an energy. It is by experiencing this energy, beyond words, that we can really understand the true orientation of the rite we practice. We can also use a discreet sound anchor to recall the entire lodge to self-remembering. Invention is welcome in this field since habit is the enemy of increased consciousness. To live in increased consciousness is to live every moment as totally new and unique. It is to realize at each working an original ritual, completely new and impossible to repeat.

What do you mean by "initiatory performance"?

At a certain stage of the work, so that the ritual does not become a new prison, to avoid an almost superstitious relationship to the ritual, to grasp that everything is ritual, that what makes the sacred gesture and word lies in us and not in the object, it is good to try initiatory performances, just as there are artistic performances. We can improvise a ritual. We can conduct a ritual in an unusual place, forest, cemetery, public dump, brothel, prison, palace, hospital, street… We can build a ritual from extracts of reference works, Cervantes, Rabelais, Dante or Shakespeare, Mozart, Michelangelo, or closer to us, Pessoa, Borges, Kazantzakis, to name just a few sacred triangles. We can build a ritual by taking a painting by Salvador Dali, Lima de Freitas, or Willem de Kooning as a tracing board… I feel perplexed. Rituals are not revealed texts. Everything written, even inspired, is born of a human brain. A ritual is not a mystery. The "mystery" lies in the poetry of language that can trigger the lightning of consciousness. We believe that we think language but it is language that thinks us. Building a ritual demystifies this game and helps us to realize that we are at the same time the producers, the directors, the stage managers, and the actors of our own show. These experiences, which must not become a new habit or a new game, make it possible to move from a conscious subjectivity to a true co-creativity.

While regularity and permanency are constitutive of the initiatory setting, habit is a fierce enemy of enlightenment. Before performing repetitive things as if it were the first time each time, one must learn to escape the dark net of memory. To "crack" the perverse influence, the instructor must know how to create surprise or dazzle, wonder or bewilderment. The initiatory performances contribute here. Too many surprises, however, install a new habit. The effectiveness of the surprise is determined by the relevance of the moment, the accuracy of the intensity, and the precision of the surprising form chosen. More than a science, it is a difficult art.

You distinguish or even oppose initiatory societies and initiatory ways. Can you clarify this distinction?

Initiatory societies are human creations that reflect our beliefs, our adaptations to the environment, our relationship to history. They are largely determined by the context in which they appear and the real motivations, conscious or unconscious, of the founders and their followers. They are always a temporary answer and we see how old organizations, institutions several decades or centuries old, become unable to understand those who come to them or accompany them in an initiatory approach when they do not know how to change their forms. They are, at best, traditional conservatories. Their function is more historical and cultural than initiatory. What's more, the "aging" process of an initiatory society is faster today in an accelerating world that risks a speeding accident at every moment.

The real ways are written in our original nature. They are not conditioned by culture, by geography, or by history. They emerge in the individual, in the heart of silence, as a pure creative energy that must learn to know and find its stride.

An initiatory society can be the temporary vessel of a way, in that it provides an environment adapted to its expression, and that it preserves the modalities of implementation. In reality, however, because every human being is unique, a particular path is destined for him and, ideally, an initiatory school should be created for every human being. Initiatory societies are thus compromises that can be useful when they are well understood. They can become harmful if, instead of being at the service of their members, they work to put the members in their service. Thus, for example, an initiatory school cannot exclusively keep members for decades.

If, metaphorically, an initiatory way is a very long road, in order to cross this road it will take several types of vehicles, car, plane, boat, horse, donkey, in all cases to finish alone, and on foot, the final ascent. The initiate will feel the need to change vessels or even types of vessels. Thus, he will abandon the lodge work for more specific work in a lineage. All this is a question of rhythm, not of opportunity. Work on the axis enacts an implementation here including traditional forms in which the initiate is embedded.

A path can be seen as emergent energy within silence. It is then enough to follow it in its verticalization. This creative energy will move and rise either by intervals (direct ways) or by more or less dense forms (magical ways), by intensifying consciousness (direct ways) or by extending it (magical ways) up to to the ultimate realization of the "point of totality." In this work, words are powerless.

It is the various perceptions of the thrill of the Real that constitute a new language.

A path is inevitably recognized by the force of its emergence in the individual, the upheavals that it produces in his psyche, and in the creative freedom that accompanies it, a vital need for the feeling of silence and isolation for the assimilation of nature and the orient. He who is seized by the way is no longer part of the world. He is "condemned" to go through it to the end, even if this fundamental injunction can seemingly take an infinite number of paths in the world of forms.

What are the different types of ways?

There is always danger in drawing typologies. Let's take the risk again. Every being, as a point of the Great Reality through which the ebb and flow of totality is manifested, is the way. So many beings, so many ways.

However, tradition distinguishes them in large groups. We could talk about the ways of action, the ways of energy, the ways of Being, the ways of the Absolute, and the non-ways.

- The ways of action arise from the desire to free oneself from the disorders of the person, of temporality, of corporality, and of number. It is a direct action against the ego or the person and against the obstacles to internal peace.
- The ways of energy consist in withdrawing the stretched energy of manifestation within one's own consciousness in order to intensify it and orient it vertically. It requires awareness of the identity of the energy of the world with one's own energy to track the intervals between two breaths, two thoughts, two gestures, and so on.
- The ways of Being, just as the ways of the Absolute, are those of the origin and of the state of total freedom from which everything flows spontaneously. These are ways of

"let it be." Let the divine act spontaneously or let go of the momentum of the Real, let oneself be invaded. According to the quality of freedom and bliss that accompanies it, we shall speak of the ways of Being or of the Absolute. If it is about "the freedom of beauty" or "the freedom of the feminine," the way of Being itself is seen in consciousness and if it is about "the freedom of art" or "the freedom of will," the Absolute will be recognized as the way. All these terms correspond to particular states. They are accurately described by Meister Eckhart or the Beguines as well as Abhinavagupta or Nagarjuna.

- Finally, there are the non-ways, the immediate wonderment of the total identity of "I am" with the Absolute. It is the Art of doing nothing, of doing No-thing, of the freedom of freedom.

What factors do you think are causing the current breakdown of the initiatory milieu?

No doubt there are many determinants of this situation. This deserves genuine study. I can only state in this regard generalities, not truths.

We live in an era dominated by the merchant caste. Our decision-makers, financial or political, are great traders. Thus, they envisage war only for mercantile reasons while hoping that it does not last in order to resume commercial exchanges as soon as possible. We are very far from the art of war and the spirit of the wars of freedom.

The world of initiation is not immune to commodification except in its terminal aspects which are elusive and thus not subject to any negotiation. For the merchant caste, all that has form can be sold. If babies, women, workers, slaves, intellectual works, and freedoms can be considered as products, why would there be any scruples to sell regalia, grades, initiatory ceremonies, "secret" rituals, etc.? The acceleration of commodification in and of the environment has led to a rapid breakdown of the initiatory milieu in recent decades. Today, the great Masonic or related obediences and the great spiritualistic or traditional movements, having become actual institutions, prisoners of political and economic imperatives of profitability and expansion, cannot propose to all their members a real initiatory program, for that would scare away the majority of them and would lead to a serious financial crisis or even bankruptcy of the organization.

Moreover, there are many leaders or staff of these organizations who live off initiation, some completely, others partially with many secondary benefits. However, any dependent relationship must be excluded.

This situation denies the liberating nature of initiation and harms the initiatory process. Everyone can observe the toxic effects of this intrusion, already very old but which seems to reach now a paroxysm, of what is most profane, trade, in the field of the sacred.

In initiation, only that which is conquered by oneself, with oneself, and in oneself, is operative. What is given to us is inoperative. All the more so, what is sold to us.

You seem to suggest sometimes that there is no transmission. Can you develop this point?

There is an excessive growth of "transmission" in the West. Initiation should be a transmission of the highest importance. I think that the excessive insistence on an indispensable transmission is often a way of taking, maintaining, or extending power over individuals or a traditional institution. If "I am the Absolute," what do I need to transmit? To summarize: the person, by definition, is not initiatable. What would it be like to initiate a plethora of false concepts? Being, or God, or the Great Architect of the Universe, or the Absolute, or the Real, or the Great Nothing (the word does not matter, as one must remember that the word is distinct from what is designated by the word),[25] has no need. The way is an unveiling of Being. It is not there to receive but to remove. To remove successive layers of sediment from the person. To render Being, the Immutable, That which remains, bare.

The completed initiation is the integral inscription in the verticality of Being. This completeness requires no transmission. It is our own nature, our own essence. Everyone has access to the Real here and now, of their own free will, without the intervention of a third party mediator.

So, what can we transmit? Not a knowing-Being, that one is indelibly engraved in the individual (the "part of God" perhaps) but, possibly, tools and know-how. The word "instructing" would be more appropriate, associated with that of companionage. It makes a companion, of all companions of adventure ("All men are my masters") an "instructor."

Of course, this does not exclude the importance of meetings. We all have a personal pantheon of individuals who have mattered or who matter on the path. They are aspects or extensions of our reality. To consider that there is a transmission is to maintain oneself in duality, in separation, and in temporality. There is no transmission in the One and the timeless!

---

25 "The map is not the territory" or "The word is not the object designated by the word." First Axiom of the General Semantics of Alfred Korzybski, a very interesting discipline from the point of view of initiation.

Do you think that the therapeutic function is really within the competence of initiatory societies?

Some initiatory societies are therapeutic. They are not of the Masonic type. With regard to Masonic or related orders, we should never accept, even in an external structure, a person in trouble. Such a person requires the skills of a psychotherapist or a psychiatrist. On the other hand, an external initiatory society has a reconciling function. It attempts to help the person to reconcile with herself, her environment, the world, her world. We presuppose that it is easier to approach the quest when the person is stabilized, when the "me" is built. Before undoing the person, it must be completed. However, all the traditions of the world present, even exhibit, counterexamples of what I have just expressed. Unbalanced people can be excellent questers and can even become saints or awakened ones, but this is not the case generally.

Now from another angle, initiation does not consist in making the prison of the "me" tolerable or in enhancing the person. It should not be confused with personal development. Initiation consists, whatever the means, of freeing oneself from the person, of leaving the prison, even if the prison has no opening (the "vicious circle" of René Daumal and the *Grand Jeu*).[26]

Another aspect of the question can be taken into account, that of the group. A lodge reacts badly to the arrival of an unbalanced person. It is a catalyst, a dynamizer of potential dysfunctions in the group.

The question is therefore complex and the answer must be adjusted to each situation.

---

26 Read on this subject the fascinating work of Marc Thivolet, *La crise du Grand Jeu* (La Bégude de Mazenc, Fr: Arma Artis, 2005).

You have suggested that some psychotic states may not be far removed from the experience of awakening. Can you explain this?

Again, beforehand, let us recall a necessary prudence toward the word "awakening" and even more about "the experience of awakening." What we call "awakening" is neither an awakening nor an experience, it is only for convenience that we use these words. The "person" has experiences or makes experiences. Awakening is a non-experience. When the "person" ceases to have and to do, it leaves room for Being. Being is the awakening.

Regarding psychotic states, it is good to note in the work of the anti-psychiatric movement in the years 1960-1970 which indeed showed the possible relations between these two non-processes.

Awakening can destroy the person and literally burn him. It can also deconstruct the person in such a way that he can no longer handle the environment effectively. Some psychotic states seem close to so-called states of awakening. The psychic apparatus is not sufficiently prepared to support, then integrate, the formidable shock of the Real. Whether the penetration of the Real is sudden or spreading, it is a total upheaval that transforms the "person" into a real chaos. It can be restructured in a similar way to its previous structuring but "at a distance." It can be reorganized in a totally different way but more adapted to this intense "here and now." It can reorganize in an incomplete manner. It may not reorganize at all. The anti-psychiatric movement suggested, in some cases, that psychotic treatments should accompany, rather than medicalize. Accompany the person through the hell of disintegration so that in the depths of this chaos she touches her own unconditioned reality, her permanence, and that, slowly, she develops a new person from this immutable foundation. This descent followed by an ascent effectively recalls the experience of great Western or Eastern mystics. I think, although the idea may offend some people, that there is much to learn about initiation by studying certain psychotic states, autism, or even deafness, because they require us to question how we build and we artificially maintain that famous reality that we venerate so much and that serves us as a prison.

Similarly, some traditions use hallucinogens at key moments of the initiatory process so that the initiatable becomes aware that reality and dream are of the same nature and that, consequently, the Real is different. This is the real first step on the path of initiation.

Isn't the false search always a true search unacknowledged? Can we make it emerge, and if so, when and how?

No matter how you start, said Aleister Crowley, the main thing is to start, even if it's black magic. We wouldn't necessarily go that far, but it is true that we can consider that what is important is that the subject knock on the door of the temple even if it is for a "bad" reason from the common point of view.

Whoever seeks power, even through war, whoever kills, rapes, or loots, seeks the same thing as us: peace, serenity or rather tranquility (l prefer this word as an echo of Fernando Pessoa), the permanence of Being, rather than the agitation and suffering of the person. His paths are plainly unsuitable, but he cannot distinguish better ones, and cannot even imagine them. Any living organism always makes the best choice among those it sees at its disposal. Whoever is led to kill has seen his choices be reduced to an alternative, kill or be killed himself. The first function of therapeutic work is to broaden the choices of the subject. A major function of initiation remains to make the individual a creator. Therefore, the initiate avoids being locked into binary alternatives. The initiate is always at the center of an infinity of possible paths. Wherever he goes, he is the way.

Behind all "bad" reasoning, bad from a moral or social point of view, there is always a being who calls. You have to know how to hear it. To hear the subject does not mean to satisfy the immediate desires of the subject but, by word, in particular metaphor, by acting on the situation, by surprise, then especially by practices, to make the true search in the conscience emerge.

The true search, that which emanates from Being, like a murmur, is never clearly audible at the beginning of the path even if the subject formulates a request which corresponds perfectly to the criteria of the initiation. It is often a "plaque" consistent with what the subject believes is expected of him. But the passage beneath the blindfold can really allow us to check if the carapace of conditioned beliefs which constitutes the person can be pierced and whether we can shake, or even move, the assembly point of "that," its tangible representation of the world.

However, the experience and the strength of the lodge must be taken into account. Some lodges cannot take the risk of accepting an individual who has no idea what he is actually looking for and who presents a pathological risk. Others are sufficiently competent and stable to welcome this subject who will benefit from real care until the moment when he will be able to engage in conscience on an initiatory path.

You seem to question the current meaning of the word "symbolism." What is the initiatory scope of symbolism?

In the field of initiation, the symbol does not represent a concept, it is an element of the alphabet of the Real. Its use applies directly to the world of energies without passing through the word. As long as the symbolic apparatus takes into account only the signifier, the meaning, and the particular referent, ritual or traditional science have no efficacy of their own. But this triangulation, of which we are content in our Aristotelian relationship to language, makes a fourth point, the metaphysical referent. In it, the first three find their unity and their bond. This metaphysical referent is fundamental. It is that which makes the sign a real symbol. As its name indicates, the metaphysical referent does not belong to the explicit world but to the implicit world. It is of transcendent order. It is the energy of which the symbol testifies. It is the archetype whose signifier, meaning, and particular referent are only distinct manifestations. I refer you to the works of Denis Labouré who synthesized in an excellent way the research of Jean Borella[27] to deepen this point of primary importance which has a direct application to the construction of the Masonic boards.[28]

---

27 Read in particular the chapter "Quand le monde devient plat" from the book *Cours Pratique d'Astrologie,* by Denis Labouré (Escalquens, Fr: Chariot d'Or, 2004). Once you have studied this synthesis, you will be able to approach two books by Jean Borella that thoroughly explore this question: *Histoire et théorie du symbole* (Lausanne: L'Age d'Homme, 2004) and *La crise du symbolisme religieux* (Lausanne: L'Age d'Homme, 1990).

28 According to Denis Labouré, this is what a board must contain that is a doorway to a symbol:

A physical description of the object concerned. If it is a tool, what is it for? What is its function in the art of building?

What does this object make me think of? I go beyond the form of the tool to access its meaning.

The function of this tool expresses a metaphysical referent (a meaning and identity that exist beyond any form) that I also express. How does the initiate on the path that is me express this meaning, this metaphysical referent? What practices does this metaphysical referent teach me?

During the entire preparation of his board, the initiate will have lived in the intimacy of this tool. Mutations will occur in his existence. What in his life expresses the same metaphysical referent will be realigned and activated. Because artisinal initiation is based on the fact that we are composed of the same metaphysical referents as those expressed by the tools, the Supervisor must carefully choose the symbol that will be worked by the apprentice or journeyman.

Does imitation have a function in the initiatory process?

The ritual work is based on imitation, on a *pretense*, which would in no way be a show. We know the importance of imitation in the martial arts, the imitation of Christ, or the imitation of Elias Artista. Integrating the form can lead to the integration of the principle provided that from one form to another we work on the same principle.

The *pretense* may allow the acquisition of a quality or skill. Pretending to possess such a quality, not vis-à-vis others for the impression, but under one's own conscious gaze, can gradually install the desired quality. This applies to qualities such as serenity or detachment. The *pretense* is futile if it is not associated with practices of self-remembering, silence, or meditation on emptiness.

You seem to use the terms "person," "me," "ego," and "mental" equivalently. Should we not distinguish them?

In this model and approach, it is not necessary to make distinctions that would only complicate things. "Person," "me," "ego," and "mental" are synonymous. They have the meaning of "troubled and disturbing mask of conditionings." It may be useful to clarify perhaps that the mind is a tool that is taken for an entity. We have access to two ways of thinking, a perceptive way of thinking, "I perceive the environment and the universe," and an analytical way of thinking, "I *speak of* the environment and the universe." Our ways of life have led us to hypertrophy analytic thought and atrophy perceptual thought, to the point that we confuse a simple activity with our deep nature. Faced with the hypertrophy of the mind, we prefer the old wisdom of the body.

You've use the qualifier "unconscious" several times. What unconscious do you speak of?

It is not a question of the Freudian unconscious, otherwise happily abused nowadays by the unconscious of neuropsychology. In agreement with Gilles Deleuze, we will say that the unconscious of which we speak is never the unconscious, the true unconscious is the Real.

When we speak of the unconscious, it is rather a pre-consciousness accessible by the attention. We should also speak of several pre-consciousnesses: a cognitive pre-consciousness that creates all that is perceived, memorized, and learned under the threshold of consciousness, an archaic pre-consciousness forged by thousands of years of evolution, and a social pre-consciousness born from the internalization of norms, values, criteria, and social habits. The "Freudian pre-conscious" around the question of the repression of sexual impulses would then be only a piecemeal and partial vision of the play of interactions between the three pre-consciousnesses: cognitive, archaic, and social.

What matters to us on the initiatory level is that we can become aware of these conditions and even "speak" of them, but we do not access the Real, the true unconscious, and we do not "speak" of it either. The Real seizes us as soon as we allow it to invade us. The experience of the Real is integral. It somehow cancels the previous experiences by absorbing them and any future experience is melted in the ecstasy or instinct of the Real, "at that moment, in this immediacy."

What is the true nature of the work of a venerable master or leader of an initiatory group?

To lead the destinies of a group for a time, whether it be a lodge, an obedience or an order, is never an honor. Remember that from the traditional point of view, as soon as we appoint a leader, as soon as an individual self-proclaims as responsible, we enter into decadence. We enter into decadence as soon as we affect the absolute freedom of Being.

Conducting the work of a team in the traditional setting is undoubtedly a responsibility. It is chiefly an exercise, an exercise in solitude. The work of self-remembering, of presence, develops the solitude of the individual and his radiance. Around him, the elements are at best set up for a creative experience in which everyone can flourish and discover unsuspected aspects of himself. In Freemasonry, during a truly solar mastership, all the members of the lodge benefit from the works in the shared moments. The exercise of the mastership makes it possible to measure our capacity with increased consciousness, with execution, and with fluidity. For a group leader, it is always interesting to take responsibility for what happens and especially failures, including when, obviously, the failure seems to originate quite beyond his doing. This is another side of the exercise of solitude, the dark side, the one that allows one to move quickly toward the non-conditioned. Of course this conscious decision to assume the totality of what happens in the field of consciousness generates creative change only if the subject is freed from the unbearable guilt of the person or knows at least to recognize the perfidy. The person never separates from a feeling of guilt, a form of giving-up and self-pity.

Isn't your approach marginal and elitist?

It cannot be described as marginal. It is central and essential. It aims at the heart of initiation and not its peripheries or vicissitudes. It is certainly a minority view but it is not isolated. Many researchers have similar or complementary requirements. A few names come to my mind: Robert Amadou, Robert Ambelain, Jean Tourniac, Jean Verdun, Alain Pozarnik, Irène Mainguy, Jean Mourgues, Jean-Pierre Sacchi, Denis Labouré among others, without forgetting all the anonymous people who leave no written trace.

The elitist reproach is inadmissible when initiation is a question of will, unconditional commitment, and work. Everyone has access to the book but, in any generation, only a few people know how to deal with the essence of literature because they put in the necessary effort. It is the same in the field of initiation. Everyone can enter the temple but most of the initiates sit at the entrance and only very few traverse the temple.

Does initiation have a political function?

Clearly and definitely, no! Even if many political movements are born of the action or the influence of spiritualistic or initiatory societies, I think of communist movements, federalists, or anarchists in particular.

Initiation is a quest for Being. Politics is a concern and an occupation of the person. That initiation modifies the view placed on the world and the mechanisms of human regulation is incontestable, but it is only a consequence, never an objective. The more the seeker advances on the path of initiation, the more the farce of the world appears to him, and politics today stands out as the farce of farces.

Initiation is liberatory. If one considers that decadence begins with the appointment or self-proclamation of a leader, this does not mean that the initiate has to cut himself off from politics. He can participate but not be identified. It is exceedingly difficult in our exacerbated era. Those who risked it were crushed. Claude Bruley[29] asserted that this farce only serves to lead us to understanding, and warned against the political temptation. It's always a personal appreciation. "Personal," I insist.

---

29 Author of numerous works leading to secular spirituality. Claude Bruley, a too little known thinker, left a work for the time to come.

Is this quest for silence and emptiness not of a nihilistic nature?

The emptiness which, for example, Meister Eckhart spoke of, who assimilated God and nothingness, is not the more or less desperate and hopeless void that the person can feel. The nature of everything is emptiness. It is the nature of Being, but this emptiness is fullness, quietude, tranquility... It is a void of intense totality made of an absolute presence without possible absence. It is the place of Being.

Transitional Conclusion

> "The ellipsis makes me shrug my shoulders out of pity. Does one need this to prove that one is a man of spirit, that is to say an imbecile? As if clarity wasn't as good as vagueness, where punctuation is concerned!"
>
> ISIDORE DUCASSE—Comte de Lautréamont. *Poems II.*

WE SOMETIMES WONDER IF FREEMASONRY can still be, or become again, initiatory? Perhaps it would be useful to ask in advance if it ever was, if there is not a great confusion about the initial Masonic project, and if we do not expect more from Freemasonry than what it can offer? Perhaps the answer to these questions is ultimately irrelevant. Indeed, Freemasonry remains a formidable potential tool of work by the setting that it guarantees. A successful transplant of the initiatory process seems quite feasible. It was attempted with relative and temporary success on some small Masonic units. It has also failed in larger units. It appears that there is a contradiction between quantity and initiation on the one hand, and between enduring form and initiation on the other. Quantity, a large quantity, participates in profanation. The pursuit of the maintenance of forms progressively mortgages the requirements of the initiatory process. The survival and development of an organization becomes the priority at the expense of the quality of work. A medium-term initiatory project, an evaluable process, can be implemented by a traditional form the ephemeral character of which is recognized and affirmed from the beginning.

A CIREM survey[30] launched in 2000 with Freemasons from various French-speaking obediences has yielded interesting results. The answers showed that a majority of sisters and brothers expected from their obedience an initiatory design and support, that it was a priority even if, for more than half of them, the social and humanist project was adjacent to it. The responses also indicated that sisters and brothers were waiting for a practice, at both personal and lodge levels, and that a growing number, without renouncing their initial Masonic commitment for the most part, were turning to smaller and more closed Masonic obediences, and towards Buddhism, Orthodoxy, martial arts... to find the pragmatic axis likely to lead them beyond the columns.

The examination of the results of the investigation also tended to show that the leaders of great obediences did not hear this request, unlike leaders of small obediences, even if the latter did not always know how to answer it.

The site is open to construction or reconstruction of a Masonic initiatory process. While some lines have been highlighted in these pages, it is neither exhaustive nor sufficient as the necessary "rectification" is considerable. It is probable, however, that it can only be through the quality and the initiatory relevance of the work of the lodges, which remain sovereign, and not by the decision of the governing bodies of obediences, rites, or orders, that Freemasonry can find a place in the world of initiation.

---

30 Survey "Quelle Franc-maçonnerie pour le XXIe siècle?" launched by the journal *L'Esprit des Choses,* conducted by the International Center for Martinist Research and Studies (CIREM) and operated by the European Masonic Observatory. CIREM deals with Martinism in the broad sense and consequently the Rectified Scottish Rite and Egyptian Freemasonry whose history is closely related to that of Martinism and Martinist orders.

In many Eastern orders and some rare Western orders, the disciples,[31] those who follow the traditional discipline, practice ten, fifteen, or twenty years of meditation on emptiness and asceticism before accessing the esoteric doctrine to implement it. Benevolence,[32] Magic,[33] theurgy, and alchemy are performed in and from the central void, the silent garden, as a celebration of strength, beauty, and wisdom.

On the contrary, the degradation and dilution of Western orders led to an inversion of this sequence. Some researchers struggle in vain with magic, theurgy, and alchemy only to finally give up, disenchanted. Some of them eventually commit to the search for silence following this cruel disillusionment. Others, the most numerous, lose themselves in their social, political, or spiritual chimera, in an exclusively intellectual approach, or in the search for power and honors.

It is, however, in silence and emptiness that the word can be creative and that Being in freedom can re-enchant the world, in creating another, without ever identifying with its creations, to live in poetry.

A Masonic and post-Masonic practice destined for large and small Masonic obediences, for wild lodges, for clandestine lodges, for orders open to Master Masons, or for orders related to one form or another of Freemasonry, will first be a practice of silence.

---

31 By this is not meant the idea of submission to a "master," but of engaging in the mastery of a discipline.

32 Benevolence can be understood as a vigil of creative harmony in the game of consciousness and energy. According to Robert Amadou, benevolence performs the same function within the system of the Rectified Scottish Rite as theurgy in the system of the Order of Knight Masons Elus Coëns of the Universe.

33 Giordano Bruno offers several definitions of magic of which one is as an art of memory.

Three Initiatory Vignettes

"The first principles must be beyond question."
ISIDORE DUCASSE—Comte de Lautréamont. *Poems I.*

YOU WILL FIND BELOW three different vignettes, which are not models but are significant experiences applying certain principles stated in this book. Some are recent, others older. We could have borrowed illustrations from other currents. The choice made, being arbitrary, is therefore not exclusive.

The first illustration covers the passage beneath the blindfold. The ritual used, which respects the landmarks of Freemasonry, introduces the possibility of making the passage beneath the blindfold the "first initiation" to the Real through appropriate questioning. The questions retained in this case are taken from actual situations but do not constitute anything like a model. They are at most an indication of the working principles.

The second illustration is an excerpt from the *Working Proposals for a Lodge of the Egyptian Rite* that were first adopted and applied in several research lodges of the Great Adriatic Sanctuary of the Ancient and Primitive Oriental Rite of Misraim and Memphis and then within various Masonic obediences of Egyptian rites. Other lodges, practicing other rites, then adapted them to their specifications.

The third illustration is a practice of ascension as performed in

Egyptian rites, this time specifically in the Egyptian High Masonry of the rite of Cagliostro.

These three cases show the same desire to emphasize the initiatory work, the free spirit of the quest rather than the always heavy traditional forms. There is nothing spectacular in this but only the search for a fine articulation between the functions, a respect of the nesting of the frames, a strong affirmation of the reality of initiation, and an invitation for an entry not delayed in a true journey.

Interviewing a Candidate Beneath the Blindfold

The following questions are intended to help the lodge to conduct the passage beneath the blindfold effectively. These are suggestions that the Venerable Master will adapt to each case.

V∴M∴: My brothers and sisters, the agenda calls for the interviewing of the candidate beneath the blindfold... At the previous meeting, we read the inquiry reports and voted on their conclusions. I remind you so that you ask your questions knowingly.

Reminder of the findings of the inquiry reports.

My brothers and sisters, do you have any additional information to add, observations to make?

The floor is given to the brothers and sisters who ask for it.

First Supervisor: Silence reigns on both columns, Venerable Master.

V∴M∴: My brothers and sisters, I remind you of the rules that preside over a passage beneath the blindfold. The Venerable Master gives the floor to the brothers and sisters who ask for it by raising their hands. A brother or sister will not ask two successive questions but may ask several questions during the interview. When the candidate answers the question, the questioning brother thanks him. This act of politeness closes the question and allows us to move on to the next.

The passage beneath the blindfold has several objectives:

Establish whether the candidate is able to speak "truly" and lucidly about himself, without eluding questions or answering what he supposes is expected of him.

Check if the candidate can benefit from the initiatory approach that we propose. Can the stone be cut? A candidate holding extremist positions or a candidate unable to hear what the other tells him would waste his time among us.

Detect if the layman is a troublemaker. There are people who, in good faith, sow discord wherever they go. We cannot take the risk of accepting them.

Push the layman into his entrenchments to bring out the "innate knowledge" from him. The interview session must be the revealer of the knowledge that the candidate carries within himself. He must come out of the test having perceived that all knowledge resides in him, but that an external facilitator is necessary for him to give birth to it. "Know yourself and you will know the universe and the gods" is the reason the passage beneath the blindfold exists.

V∴M∴: We will proceed to the interview of the candidate… Brother Master of Ceremonies, remove your regalia and look for the candidate in the forecourt. Blindfold him. You will introduce him without ceremony and have him sit between the columns.

It is done. Meanwhile…

V∴M∴: My brothers and sisters, any dialogue with the candidate is forbidden. You will ask to speak by raising your hand and waiting for me to signal you to ask your question.

Interviewing a Candidate Beneath the Blindfold

Brother Master of Ceremonies introduces the candidate. Silence.

V∴M∴: Good evening M., do not be surprised at the formalities and inquiries to which you are subjected. All admissions to our lodge are subject to the same rules. If you are admitted among us, they will be for you a guarantee of the quality of the human beings that you will meet there and the works that are conducted there. Some do not know you, and we all need to know who you really are. Following your application for admission, you were visited by three of us. Today, we invite you to answer the questions from all the brothers and sisters who wish to question you. At the end of this interview, everyone will decide on your application for admission. Know that our conclusion will be based on your sincerity and not on your opinions.

Beforehand, we ask of you a commitment of honor: to reveal nothing of what you have been able to see or hear since you sent your application and to reveal nothing of what you will be able to see or hear during the inquiries or interviews of which you will be the object. Do you so promise?

Candidate: I do.

V∴M∴: M... I take note of the promise you have just made.

Silence.

V∴M∴: Before beginning our interview, I shall tell you that the lodge into which you ask to be admitted is devoted to initiatory work. If you wanted to enter this Masonic Lodge to gain relationship or professional benefits, you could only be disappointed. M..., can you briefly tell us the motives that led you to apply for admission to our Masonic lodge?

Candidate's answer.

V∴M∴: Thank you M..., what is your biggest fault?

Candidate's answer.

V∴M∴: Thank you M..., what is your best quality?

Candidate's answer.

The Venerable Master gives the floor to the brothers and sisters who ask for it. Here are some examples of questions from passages beneath the blindfold that were for the future initiate a real discovery of the artificial nature of the person. In no case should these examples, taken out of context, be taken as a model. They are only illustrations of our remarks.

M..., what do you call **freedom?**

Candidate's answer.

M..., what do you mean by "x"? (*Take a nominalization or qualifier in the answer, for example, if the candidate answers, "It's an inner feeling," ask him, "What do you mean by* feeling?" *And then "What do you mean by* inner?" *Continue until the speech is exhausted The candidate must grasp that the words are oriented, right, left, front, behind... but are intrinsically meaningless.*)

Objective: Make the candidate aware of language's inability to grasp and report on the Real.

M..., how do you know you exist?

Objective: To get the candidate from "why?" to "how?" Do not let him answer a "why" question when the question is phrased "how," which we do very frequently so as not to get into the deep layers of the psyche. The answer to "why?" is always a representation. The answer to "how?" has a verifiable sensory base. On several occasions during the hearing, it will be interesting to ask the question "How do you know?" following a response from the candidate.

M..., are you conscious?

Candidate's answer: yes.

Yet, your hands move without you noticing, you are not aware of your buttocks on the chair, or the soles of your feet on the floor, etc. M..., are you conscious?

Objective: To give a foreboding of the problem of consciousness.

M..., what is the meaning of life?

Objective: To collect the values and criteria of the conditioned person.

M..., what is the meaning of your life?

Objective: Break the generalization. To pass from concepts to the lived experience.

    A response such as "My daughter" is obviously preferable to the offer of a response such as "The good of humanity."

M..., if you had a choice between these four ways to awaken: war, thieving, sex, or gambling, which of these four ways would you choose?

Objective: To get the candidate out of a strategy of maintaining a "good" image of himself, to take the risk of an unexpected and perhaps subversive verbal and non-verbal response from his point of view, but a more significant one.

M..., what are your conditionings?

Objective: See above. In addition, there is an indication of the nature of initiatory work. It is interesting to ask the same question several times at various points in the interview.

    The next question, apparently more understandable, pursues the same objective.

M..., can you tell us what in the experience of your life is your own and what is the other's?[34]

M..., can you give us a list of your fears?

Candidate's answer.

M..., can you classify them in three categories: the fears that you think you can easily control, the ones you think you can master over time, and the ones you think you can never control?

Objective: To determine if the candidate is sufficiently lucid about himself and available for deep work.

M..., if you are received in the temple, what will this change in your family, social, professional life?

Objective: Verification of the candidate's ecology.

We know the case, certainly extreme, of a magistrate who asked for admission to a Masonic lodge. There were no inquiries. "Is it right to investigate a magistrate?" It is indeed delicate but a conversation or interview with a magistrate, even three of them, does not present difficulties. There was no passage beneath the blindfold. "You understand, we cannot put a blindfold on the eyes of the magistrate and in any case the passage beneath the blindfold is useless because we cannot refuse him." The magistrate appointed the date and the time of his own initiation. When the day arrived, it meant that he had to depart after 90 minutes. The initiation was expedited and the ceremony truncated. Subsequently, for professional reasons, he could not attend the meetings and eventually disappeared into the wild. The magistrate is not to blame for this disaster. It was the lodge and its Venerable Master who were unable to guarantee the setting. The pro-

---

34 On the "self" and "other," read Otto Gross, "On the Inferiority Complexes," in *Selected Works 1901-1920* (Hamilton, NY: Mindpiece, 2012), pp. 173-255.

fessional ecology of this magistrate did not allow him to engage in a Masonic approach.

Note that if the concept of "counter-initiation" were ever admissible, it would be apt in this situation. In this case we are in the opposite of initiation, a simple opposite rather than a hypothetical Guénonian counter-initiation. In fact, initiation either is or is not. René Guénon's concept of counter-initiation is quite wrong, often damaging, and terribly dualistic.

M…, on the chessboard, what piece are you?

Candidate's answer.

M…, on the chessboard, which piece do you want to become?

Candidate's answer.

Objective: Find representations of the present state and the desired state.

Once no one asks for the floor, or if the V∴M∴ judges that the interrogation has lasted long enough:

V∴M∴: M…, diligence and respect for commitments are two important aspects of our rule. Know right now that you would have to participate in two meetings a month that are currently taking place on… *(indicate the day of the week).* If you were accepted among us, do you commit to the brothers and sisters gathered here to respect this assiduity?

Candidate's answer.

V∴M∴: M…, you will not be able to evaluate a spiritual path without having seriously tried it. Are you ready to give the Masonic method a chance by trusting us? While waiting three full years before making a judgment on the effectiveness of our teachings and our practices?

Candidate's answer.

V∴M∴: M..., we will remember your answers tonight if need be. We thank you for your answers and the goodwill you have put in us to make them. You will withdraw and we will keep you informed of the follow-up that will be given to this interview. We remind you of your promise of silence on everything you will be able to see or hear as a result of your admission request to our lodge. Please see out M....

After the departure of the candidate and the return of Brother Master of Ceremonies.

V∴M∴: My brothers and sisters, you have heard the answers of the candidate to your questions. Do you have any comments? The floor will be given to each of you to express yourself and give your conclusions.

The Venerable Master asks for the conclusion of each member of the lodge. At the end of the comments:

First Supervisor: Silence reigns on both columns, Venerable Master.

V∴M∴: Brother Orator, please give your opinion and your conclusions for the vote, on the possible initiation of this candidate.

Orator: Given... *(he explains the conclusions he draws from the comments of the members of the lodge)*, I am favorable (*or opposed*) to the initiation of this candidate. *If he is opposed to initiation, the Brother Orator may propose an adjournment or a definitive refusal. In the first case, the procedure will be restarted after a fixed delay with the agreement of the lodge.*

V∴M∴: Brother Orator, please describe the voting arrangements for the initiation of this candidate.

Orator: According to the regulations defined by the members of this session, the votes are by show of hands, unless a master member of the lodge requests a secret ballot. To initiate or affiliate a candidate, unanimity is required. If a master votes against Brother Orator's conclusions, he gives the reasons to the other members.

After the vote...

V∴M∴: The candidate is... admitted (*or refused or adjourned to... specify the delay*).

Working Proposals for a Lodge of the Egyptian Rite

Objectives for the first three degrees

The lodge work is a weaving. This weaving has a triple dimension: physical (motor), psychic (intellectual and emotional), and spiritual. The patterns of this weaving differ with each dimension. The lodge will provide the tools to successively access the three stages of the journey: exoteric, mesoteric, and esoteric. Let us recall what those are.

Exoteric

(*Apprentice*) The goal of this step is therapeutic. It strives to restore for the initiate the refocusing and alignment of body, emotion, and thought. It is about reconciling the initiate with himself and with his environment. The initiate is invited to study and integrate a model of the world described as "spiritual" that:

- brings to the great problems of life an answer satisfactory to the mind and reassuring to the heart.
- teaches him a common vocabulary with the other brothers of the lodge.

Let's take an example. The first two degrees of Freemasonry emphasize the artisanal initiation. It means that work is the support of spiritual realization. When the potential of the initiation becomes effective, it generally has the effect of transformation in the professional life of the initiate. One goes from "work" to "profession." The support of realization, which was inadequate, realigns itself so that the initiate continues his progress.

Mesoteric

(*Companion*) This stage develops in the initiate the necessary skills to effectively approach a real way. It leads him to fill the gaps of free, secular, and compulsory education. For that, he studies the foundations of the seven liberal arts. These give him the necessary tools to tackle the three hermetic sciences: astrology, alchemy, and theurgy. It is a question of experiencing the state of "Mage," the one who, expressing his true Will (and not the desires and caprices of the self), makes the universe respond. Finally, he begins the process that will lead to his regeneration.

Esoteric

(*Master*) This step introduces the initiate into a real Way (the Way of Awakening, the Way of the Body of Glory, *theosis,* etc.). At this stage of his journey, God (or the Sublime Architect of the Worlds) is perceived as a qualitative axis. The master mason, when he is actually in the middle chamber, is His reflection. Until then, he perceived himself as a physical body animated by a consciousness fed by the perceptions of the five senses. He was subject to physical and quantitative law. Having regained his identity, he demonstrates his superiority over the "physical" or "natural" laws. In all things, his universe adjusts to his true identity. This process is gradual. Pursued to the end, it would lead the master to immortality.

Whatever the degree (apprentice, journeyman or master), the work of the Freemason of the Egyptian Rite is underpinned by a key: the lodge seen as the representation of the human body. This model will guide the reflection on the work (the hermetic model in four bodies, the first approach of the body of glory).

Development of each meeting

Here are some guidelines on the form of work, common to the first three degrees.

Commitments

- a ritual meeting per month.
- obligatory agapes at the end of the meeting with a short ritual. Sharing bread and wine.
- a training session per month for apprentices and journeymen. As for the masters, they will gather together to take stock, without ceremony, on their practices, the obstacles encountered along the Way, and the proposals for progress through the operativities.

When passing beneath the blindfold, the candidate is asked to commit to his attendance at two monthly meetings. The rules having been laid down even before his initiation, chronic absenteeism will not be accepted.

When a brother cannot be present, he will directly inform the Venerable Master. If this brother is an officer, the Venerable Master will reorganize his college of officers for this particular meeting without being caught off-guard.

Contents of the meeting

Before a meeting of the rank of apprentice, the temple is installed by the Master of Ceremonies accompanied by apprentices.

Each meeting is preceded by a brief but intense work. For example:

- an aspect of the ritual. On this occasion, the Master of Ceremonies will draw attention to a point in the ritual (pos-

ture, gesture, state of presence, etc.) that the brothers will try to master during the opening and closing of the work.
- the assumption of divine forms. Especially on the *neter* from which the lodge derives its name.

At each meeting, a paper is presented by a different brother from the lodge. For apprentices and companions, it concerns a symbol present in the ritual (symbolic paper), or a virtue or a phrase extracted from the ritual (philosophical paper). If presented by an apprentice, the theme of this paper is assigned by the Junior Warden according to the interest of the lodge and the personality of the apprentice. If presented by a companion, the theme will be chosen by the Senior Warden under the same conditions. Masters are free to choose their subject.

When the brother reads his paper, no one is allowed to interrupt or disrupt him.

When the brother has finished reading his paper, each brother of the lodge intervenes to ask for a clarification or to provide a comment. In this phase of the meeting, each brother intervenes only once. There is no dialogue between two brothers. If the apprentices are allowed to intervene (only once also), the brothers will speak in such a way that they make a contribution without feeling that everything has already been said.

When this phase is over, the Speaker summarizes the interventions, being sure to highlight at least one idea presented by each of the brothers. All the more so when the contribution was made by a brother who finds it difficult to express himself orally.

When a brother apprentice or companion presents one of the two papers written for his advancement, the brothers will be severe during that phase of the meeting. It is a matter of pushing the brother to the end of his reflection, and especially of flushing out any answer that is insincere. In a way, the spiritual progression of a man is proportional to his ability not to take refuge in insincerity, and his courage to face real questions. If, however, a master breaks down the view of an apprentice or a journeyman, he will take care to lead him to another view, so that the apprentice or companion understands the vanity of the reactions and perceives the exercise behind the exercise. When the paper concerns a topic chosen freely by the brother (when it is not a paper for his advancement), the brothers will show a greater moderation. When a brother gives an experience of his own (for example when he reads "Impressions of initiation"), it will be received as such, without comments, by the entire lodge.

Training meetings

The Junior Warden organizes a monthly meeting (without ritual) of compulsory education with all the apprentices. The Senior Warden does the same with the companions. This meeting has for its triple function the cohesion between the apprentices (or the companions), the teaching of Masonic theory, and introduction to the practices. Wardens are not accountable to anyone for their teaching. However, experience shows that the following model can be used in most instructions:

- one-third of the time is spent studying the ritual (symbols, phrases, philosophical concepts).
- one-third of the time is spent discussing or presenting the papers under preparation.
- one third of the time is spent on practices: the practice of presence (active recognition) for apprentices, practices of alchemy and divination for journeymen.

Second and third degree meetings

The Venerable Master will organize during the year some meetings for the ranks of companion and master. The efficient decoding of the operative procedures included in the ritual involves an overall view of the three degrees. These meetings will allow passages (advancements) and the presentation of papers specifically concerning the journeyman and master ranks.

Agapes

The agape is a meal to foster the communion of hearts. This meal begins with a ritual of sharing bread and wine. During the agape, the Venerable Master will be provided with his mallet. He will use it to obtain silence and inform the brothers of what seems important to him. To strike, he will choose the moments when a brother, wrapped in a discussion, would tend to monopolize speech. Thus, a real exchange will be restored. If necessary, the Venerable Master will give the floor to a brother. Thus, he will be able to ensure that everyone expresses himself.

Banquets of Saint John

Twice a year, near the solstices (Saint John of Winter and Saint John of Summer), a ritualized meal will be organized. If the program of the lodge allows it, it replaces the regular meeting. Otherwise, the meeting will be shortened and followed by this meal. This meal, which requires the silence of all the brothers, will be an opportunity to meditate on the food and the alchemical nature of the agape.

Affiliations

When a brother from another obedience wishes to join our lodge, it will proceed as follows:

He will regularly visit the lodge for a dozen meetings. This will give both him and us time to see if we can adopt each other.

After this time, he can formally request his affiliation. In the meantime, he will have prepared a paper to be presented at the lodge. A vote will be organized following his paper. Unanimity is required for him to be affiliated.

He will follow the instructions corresponding to his rank. If he is a master, he will nevertheless follow the instructions of apprentice or journeyman for a year, so as to acquire the knowledge possessed by the other brothers of the lodge.

According to the rules of obedience, neither the apprentice nor the companion is reinitiated. They are affiliated with the rank that was already theirs. It's different for the masters. These must traverse the Osirian elevation which is the peculiarity of our rite. It is only after this elevation that they are legitimately considered "masters of the Egyptian Rite."

Apprentice of the Craft

Form

If the candidate has made contact with the lodge by his own means and does not know any brother who is a member, the prerequisites for initiation are normal: a prior interview with the Venerable Master, three inquiries, and the passage beneath the blindfold. If the passage beneath the blindfold is favorable, a brother must propose himself as sponsor. A candidate for initiation will be initiated only if a sponsor agrees to accompany him during his course in the blue lodge (from his initiation to his accession to master). The sponsor will be the preferred interlocutor of this future initiate. If the candidate has been proposed by a brother of the lodge, this brother could be the sponsor. The procedure will follow its normal course (interview, inquiries, blindfold, etc.). It goes without saying that being a sponsor is not an administrative formality. An apprentice who does not hear from his sponsor between two meetings would be entitled to have a very poor opinion of the one who is committed to accompany him.

The Junior Warden is the only one authorized to propose the passage of an apprentice brother to the rank of journeyman. He is also solely responsible for the teaching he provides. When the Junior Warden proposes the passage of an apprentice to the rank of journeyman, the Venerable Master will dismiss the apprentices. Then the Junior Warden will explain to the lodge the reasons for his decision, specifying the nature of the progress made by the apprentice. The masters of the lodge who so wish will be able to interrogate. Then the masters will give (or not) the green light for this passage.

In the lodge, apprentices only speak when invited by the Junior Warden. Before that is possible, several months of absolute silence will pass from them.

The Junior Warden organizes an obligatory instructional meeting (without ritual) every month with all apprentices. This meeting has the triple function of cohesion between apprentices, teaching Masonic theory, and introduction to the practices.

Before the apprentice reads his paper in front of the lodge:
- he will have questioned the masters of the lodge. This allows him to benefit from acquired experience. In this way, oral transmission is passed along. The apprentice is free to retain what seems good.
- he will have already presented his paper to the other apprentices in the instructional meeting. Before the final draft, he will have taken into account the contributions and reflections made then.
- lastly, he will have presented his work to the Junior Warden, who will make such remarks as seem to him judicious. Three or four back-and-forths between the apprentice and the Junior Warden are desirable before the Junior Warden agrees to the presentation at the lodge.

The paper read in front of all members of the lodge will be the result of a process of maturation that lasted several months.

Theme: the alignment of the four bodies

Theory

Study of the ritual (the process of the rite, the installation of the temple, disposition of the officers, etc.) and the catechism of the apprentice of the Craft.

Study of a model of man in relation to the model implicit in the ritual. It can be the hermetic model of the four bodies (earth, water, air, fire). This model is present in the initiation rite in the form of the "purification by the four elements" and the four corresponding journeys. It can also be the ternary "physical center, emotional center, intellectual center" or "body, soul, spirit" present in other traditions.

Here are some themes that can be addressed in the instructions: What is a rite (the difference between rite and ceremonial)? What is a symbol (the effectiveness of the symbol, its absorption)? What is "putting oneself in order"? The different models of the rite. The officers of the lodge and their function. The different tools. Postures (standing to order, the sitting posture called "the divine forms," etc.) and the internal dimension.

Before becoming a journeyman, each apprentice brother will present two papers. One will deal with an operatively decoded symbol (the so-called "symbolic" paper), the other with a sentence of the ritual also decoded operatively (the so-called "philosophical" paper).

With the Junior Warden, the apprentices will think about the purpose of the papers. It is diverse: the integration of a model of the world possessing a therapeutic virtue, decoding tools useful for work, the observation of the reactions of the ego when its content is questioned, etc. In particular, apprentices will have to understand that being right makes no sense, but mastering oneself does.

Practices

During training sessions, the Junior Warden will train the apprentices to:
- regain their original openness by observing themselves without judgment.
- align in a healthy way the various aspects of the human being.

If the lodge uses the hermetic model of the four bodies, the function of these exercises will be to align the bodies of earth, water, air, and fire. If the lodge uses a three-body model, the function of the exercises will be to align the motor, emotional, and intellectual centers.

The exercises will aim to maintain a state of presence for the duration of the meeting. During the oral exchanges (papers, comments), this work can be reinforced by an auditory anchor (discrete strikes of the mallet by the Venerable Master).

Companion of the Craft

Form

The Senior Warden alone is authorized to propose the passage of a brother companion to the rank of master. He is also solely responsible for the teaching he provides. When the Senior Warden proposes the elevation of a companion to the rank of master, the Venerable Master will dismiss the apprentices and the companions. Then the Senior Warden will explain to the lodge the reasons for his decision, specifying the nature of the progress made by the companion. The masters of the lodge who so wish will be able to interrogate. Then the masters will give (or not) the green light for this passage.

The Senior Warden organizes an obligatory instructional meeting (without ritual) every month with all the companions. This meeting has the triple function of cohesion between companions, teaching Masonic theory, and initiation to the practices.

Before the companion reads his paper in front of the lodge:
- he will have questioned the masters of the lodge. This allows him to benefit from acquired experience. In this way, oral transmission is passed along. The companion will retain what seems good.
- he will have already presented his paper to the other companions in the instructional meeting. Before the final draft,

- he will have taken into account the contributions and reflections made then.
- lastly, he will have presented his work to the Senior Warden, who will make the remarks which seem to him judicious. Three or four back-and-forths between the companion and the Senior Warden are desirable before the Senior Warden agrees to the presentation at the lodge.

The paper read in front of all the members of the lodge will be the result of a process of maturation that lasted several months.

The companion is considered worthy of being raised to the rank of master when his natural behavior shows that he has understood one thing: it is by helping the search of another that he helps his own progression. In other words, the more a companion tries to help his brother, even if his brother's Way is different from his own, the more he understands the spirit of Masonic companionage. As long as a companion collects recipes for his own good, he will not be offered to the Masters. As long as he does not participate spontaneously in community activities (agapes, news of brothers in difficulties outside of meetings, etc.), he will not enter the Middle Chamber.

Theme: lighting the flaming star

Theory

Study of the ritual and the catechism of the companion of the Craft.

Understanding of the function of the symbol as an interface between two worlds and not simply as a medium of psychological projection.

If "the apprentice cannot read or write," the companion is trained in the handling of the tools. In any operative way, the neophyte is often perplexed by the role of secular knowledge.

True wisdom does not lie in the intellect. That is true. It is no less true that a small amount of baggage is useful for correctly understanding what is read and what is practiced. What are the useful areas of knowledge? The companion ritual answers this question. These are the seven liberal arts and the classical philosophers. They concentrate the foundations needed to enter the practice of the three hermetic sciences. The companion must acquire the basics:

- of the seven liberal arts: these break down into the *trivium* that allows one to possess language and to master logic (grammar, dialectic, rhetoric) and the *quadrivium* (arithmetic, geometry, astronomy, music) that studies the cosmic harmony through its manifestations, especially Number and Rhythm. These "seven columns of wisdom" will fill the gaps of modern-day education. For example, by studying the *trivium*, the companion will work on the art of speaking well, the mechanisms of speaking, and the conditioning that is at stake when he speaks. By studying the *quadrivium*, he will elaborate the "sphere of Ptolemy" whose understanding is indispensable to the penetration of astrology and alchemy. He will endeavor to understand the sky, to recognize the stars, regardless of what any stellar map with its instructions will impart to him. It is the same for the other liberal arts.
- of the *Trivium Hermeticum*: astrology, alchemy, and magic. For example, the companion will undertake the theoretical study of metallic alchemy: the way of cinnabar appears most easily accessed. If the lodge has an instructor in alchemy, the decoding (and practice) of the way of cinnabar will be an excellent training. If the lodge does not have an instructor in this field, the spagyric courses formerly distributed by the group "Les Philosophes de la Nature" will make

for good material. It is also possible to order the course of the Scot Adam McLean[35] who teaches how to decode alchemical imagery.

- of philosophy. From Plato, he will study the *Symposium* (prototype of the Masonic agape), the myth of the cave (the end of Book VII of the *Republic*), and the relationship between oral and written transmission (the *Phædrus*). He will remember that education is not about accumulating knowledge from outside. To educate is to remember. Every human being has the innate knowledge. Education is learning how to access it (the passage beneath the blindfold). He will understand that the world of phenomena that surrounds us is not the Real. It is the reflection, the symbol. He will see how the ascent from the world of reflection towards the pure light takes place (from the cabinet of reflection to the consecration by the Venerable Master). From Pythagoras, he will retain the quality of numbers, the symbols of the Pythagorean current (the flaming star, the number five, the bread and salt in the agape), and the rules of the brotherhood (silence, the probationary phase).

The companion will work on the five senses by trying to understand what, in perception, comes from the objective world and what from the subjective world. One brother brought us a small catalog of optical illusions!

Practice of a divinatory art involving a "symbolic keyboard" (geomancy, horary astrology, etc.). An art using seven symbols is preferable, because of its connection with the seven-branched candlestick that is at the heart of our ritual. The goal is to use a pictographic language that allows one to obtain a response from the universe.

---

35   Adam McLean, *Study Course on Alchemical Symbolism*, https://www.alchemywebsite.com/bookshop/foundation_study_course.html.

Before being raised to the rank of master, each companion brother will present two papers. One will focus on an operatively decoded symbol (the "symbolic" board), the other on a ritual phrase (the "philosophical" board).

The Senior Warden will design for each companion a travel project composed of secular and sacred places. He will have to meet people accomplishing their profession: from the icon painter to the alchemist, from the horseman to the cabinet maker. Some places will have to be disconcerting for the companion.

Practices

The companion will look for how he can concretely (we should even say "physically") light the flaming star. There are various ways to do this. One, adopted by Cagliostro, consists of "enflaming by prayer." In this context, *Le christianisme secret*[36] and *The Art of Prayer*[37] will be useful. But there are possible non-Christianizing ways, like the movement of breath in Hermeticism.

By studying the four elements and the ether, he will realize some experiments in spagyrics. These will make him physically understand what is meant by "the radical heat of the Sun," "the radical humidity of the Moon," hot and cold, dry and wet, the four elements, and the quintessence.

---

36 Denis Labouré, *Le christianisme secret—Le Corps de Lumière* (revised and expanded edition of the book *Alchimie céleste*) (Paris: Le Mercure Dauphinois, 2009).

37 Igumen Chariton of Valamo, *The Art of Prayer*, trans. E. Kadloubovsky and E. M. Palmer, ed. Timothy Ware (London: Faber & Faber, 1966).

Master of the Craft

Form

There is no instructional meeting at the rank of Master. But the lodge will meet from time to time at this rank and will deepen the indicated program.

    The master mason can continue what Yahweh replies to Moses: *"I am the one who is."* Like Jesus, he affirms in all conscience: *"Before Abraham was, I am."* Like Cagliostro, he says to his Judges: *"I am not of any time or of any place; beyond time and space my spiritual being lives an eternal existence. I turn my thoughts back over the ages and I project my spirit toward an existence far beyond that which you perceive, I become what I choose to be. Participating consciously in the Absolute Being, I arrange my actions according to what is at hand. My name defines my actions because I am free. My country is wherever my feet stand at the moment. Put yesterday behind you if you dare, like the forgotten ancestors who came before you, give no thought to the morrow and the illusionary hope of greatness that will never be yours, I will be what I am... Here I am: I am noble and a traveller; I speak and your soul trembles in recognition of ancient words; a voice within you which was killed a long time ago responds to the appeal of mine. I act, and peace returns to your hearts, health into your bodies, hope and courage into your souls."*

    The master mason is master because he is recognized as such

by his elders and the companions and apprentices he teaches. In particular, the master will be recognized as such when he will be able to present (at least orally) an operative decoding of the tracing board. Each companion will have the right to question him on the subject.

Any master answering the question of an apprentice or a companion with a phrase like "it doesn't fit your age," "you will see later" will be sentenced to pay 1€ to the Widow's Trunk.

Theme: the formation of the Body of Glory (lighting the seven-branched candlestick)

Theory

Study of the ritual and the catechism of the master of the Craft.

The basic question will be: what is the middle chamber (the vertical axis, the stabilized consciousness) from the operative point of view?

The question will be compared with the legend of Osiris. The Chamber of the masters will reflect on the difference between the myth of Osiris and that of Hiram. In the Egyptian lodge, the initiate raises *himself* as a new Osiris. In the classic lodge, Hiram, assassinated, having become a rotten corpse, is resurrected *through* the new master. Moreover, in the legend, Osiris is resuscitated by the breath of Isis. From Isis to the Virgin Mary, from the Mother of the World to Kali, the master will investigate the role of the Woman in the birth or resurrection of God.

The master will learn to distinguish the work that is done on the double body (called the "lunar body" or "astral body," depending on the school) and that which concerns the Body of Light (the Body of Glory of Christianity, the Rainbow Body of Taoism, etc.). For there lies the discrimination between the psychic and the spiritual, between the ephemeral and the timeless, between what "is" and what "passes."

The master will study the *Egyptian Book of the Dead*.[38] He will decipher the procedures of internal alchemy keeping in mind that *Amenta* (the other world, the underground world) is his body. Apparently, the *Book of the Dead* relates the journey of the dead through the other world. But these journeys also describe the processes of regeneration that unfold in his body until the man becomes a new Osiris.

The program will include the study of different cultural and traditional patterns of death and immortality. In Christianity, the master will look for the first death and then the second death. From a more global point of view, he will question the four deaths: death of the self-image, death of the human form, death "to the world," and death "of the world."

Practices

Essentially, the master will look for ways to light the seven-branched candlestick, i.e., to carry out the program expressed by this phrase pronounced at the opening of all our works: *"I pray you to perform on the altar the rite that each one of us, at this moment, will perform internally."* To understand the role of the seven-branched candlestick in internal alchemy, the master will use the images found in *Theosophia Practica*,[39] comments that have been made by Julius Evola and Bernard Gorceix, and the decoding of the first story of creation (Book of Genesis). If this has not been done, he will receive the oral instructions that

---

38 Raymond O. Faulkner (trans.) et al., *The Egyptian Book of the Dead: The Book of Going Forth by Day* (San Francisco: Chronicle, 1994).

39 Johan Georg Gichtel, *Theosophia Practica,* published in English as Arthur Versluis (trans.), *Awakening to Diving Wisdom: Christian Initiation into Three Worlds* (St Paul, MN: New Grail, 2004).

accompany the lighting of the seven-branch candlestick.

During the rite, self-remembering must be practiced by everyone as well as the integration of the rite into the breath.

The three masteries (hunger, sleep, and sexuality) will be approached gradually and implemented for the important equinoxes, solstices, and rituals. From the fasts of the four periods performed in ancient Christianity to the fasts prescribed in the hermetic currents, the master has materials to deepen the link between fasting and the cycles.

Here are some possible paths depending on the sensitivity of the master. He must work on the assumption of the divine forms (particularly the *neter* Anubis and the *neter* who watches over the lodge if it has adopted the name of a *neter*).

How to Ascend to the Upper Chamber[40]

The Temple, representation of the human body

To understand the upper chamber as the image of a higher state of consciousness is a big step. This step is nevertheless insufficient for our transmutation to take place. To understand the internal alchemy, we must go further and find the lost key.

Ever scholarly, the contemporary Freemason repeats that his lodge is a miniature society, an image of the external society. This superficial philosophy does not take him far. Who told him that he was mostly the reproduction of the human microcosm? No one. However, like the Egyptian or Hindu temples, or cathedrals, his lodge reproduces a head, arms, legs and all organs of the body. Pomegranates, symbol of fertility, in the tracing board (or the altar, depending on the Rite) placed in the center of the lodge, everything is a representation of the body. The entry and the exit of the initiates, as well as the position and the movements of the officers, instruct one on the processes of regeneration.

---

40 Document composed of excerpts from the *Cours de Haute Maçonnerie Égyptienne* by Denis Labouré, since revised and published as *Cagliostro et les arcanes du rite égyptien* (Ostwald, Fr: Spiritualité occidentale, 2011).

> *They* [the Ancients] *have conformed to the measurements of the human body to build their temples, their buildings, their houses, their theaters, their ships, their machines, and their works of art, as well as all the parts of the buildings which are like members: columns, capitals, bases, pediments and pedestals.*
>
> CORNELIUS AGRIPPA, *Celestial Magic*, Chapter 27

Martinez de Pasqually (circa 1710-1774) compares the Temple of Solomon to the body of man. The body can be divided into three parts:

- the porch for the lower limbs to the waist,
- the temple for the chest,
- the sanctuary for the head.

As for the Holy of Holies, this very mysterious fourth part of the temple is not the type of any part of the human body. But it is up to the operative to bring it in, and theurgy will help.[41]

From the upper chamber to the top of the head

The holy mountain and the middle chamber illustrate the same reality: to meet our God, we must reach the summit of ourselves. Leaving aside that, in the last stage, the veil of our flesh is torn away as a form that we escape.

The top of the head

The top of the head is the highest part of the body. The man is different from most animals by raising his head and walking upright.

In the Temple of Solomon, the room to the east was the *Debir*,

---

41 Serge Caillet, *Cours de Martinisme*, lesson VIII, 14. This question is particularly mentioned in Martinez de Pasqually, *Traité sur la réintégration des êtres*, ed. Robert Amadou (Paris: Diffusion Rosicrucienne, 2000), sections 254, 257, and 258.

or Holy of Holies. It was accessed by a winding staircase, located on the right side of the sanctuary. It was a cubic room, without a window. It housed the Ark of the Covenant. Like the Temple of Solomon, the sanctuary of the Temple of Herod included a vestibule, closed by an embroidered curtain, which overlooked the Holy Place, a cubic room of 20m on a side, containing the altar of perfumes, the table of shewbread, and the seven-branched candlestick. Between the Holy Place and the Holy of Holies, a double curtain, woven of four colors, concealed the most sacred place; it sheltered only a simple slab of stone. The Epistle to the Hebrews likens the Holy of Holies "beyond the curtain" (Heb. 6:19-20) to the sky into which Jesus entered after His ascension. When Jesus gives up the soul, the veil is torn apart.[42] Even more, the veil that is torn apart is the

---

42 Here are some details taken from Jean Borella (*Esotérisme guénonien et mystère chrétien*). There was, indeed, in the Temple, an outer veil that the Hebrew calls *masak*, separating the court of the Holy (where the ordinary liturgies were held), and an inner veil that the Hebrew calls *paroketh*, separating the Holy Place from the Holy of Holies (where the high priest only entered once a year). None of the gospels specify which veil was torn at the death of Jesus: they speak only of "the veil." It is important, however, to consider the Epistle to the Hebrews. This epistle mentions the veil of the Temple three times: 6:19; 9:3; 10:20. The first mention: *We have* [hope] *as an anchor of the soul, both sure and stedfast, and which entereth into that within the veil; Whither the forerunner is for us entered, even Jesus, made an high priest for ever after the order of Melchisedec.* Then the second veil, which the second mention specifies, describes the interior layout of the Earth Temple—a description with archetypal value rather than historical—in the following way: *And after the second veil, the tabernacle which is called the Holiest of all... Christ being come an high priest of good things to come, by a greater and more perfect tabernacle, not made with hands... entered in once into the holy place, having obtained eternal redemption for us* (9:11-12). *Mediator of the new testament* (9:15), *Christ is not entered into the holy places made with hands, which are the figures of the true; but into heaven itself* (9:24). According to the express will of the crucified Son, *we are sanctified through the offering of the body of Jesus Christ once for all* (10:10). *Having therefore, brethren, boldness to enter*

flesh—that is, the body—of Jesus Christ (Heb. 10:20).

Reading these passages with the human body in mind will aid in the understanding of the second regeneration. According to Paul, the Christian is himself the Temple of God, the sanctuary of the living God (1 Cor. 3:16-17).

The crucifixion takes place on a small hill named *Golgotha*. It is the transliteration of an Aramaic word meaning "place of the skull." In Latin, it translates as *Calvariae locus,* hence the English word *Calvary*.

From these remarks, there follows a consequence: in this corporeal Temple, the top of the head is the Holy of Holies. It is enclosed in the philosopher's gold, the most precious substance. The veil of the flesh must be torn apart for us to reach it. We must cast anchor beyond the veil of matter. The lamp that is there will be illuminated when the oil from the backbone is sufficiently refined: *"the days when God watched over me; when his lamp shined upon my head"* (Job 29:3).

Operate after rising

Where does the Egyptian Mason operate?

You are walking on a frozen lake. The ice gives way under your feet. You end up in the water, under the ice. If you try to regain the edge of the lake, you are lost. Beforehand, you must go back to the surface and hoist yourself over the ice. Only then can you return to the bank.

The scriptures compare "rising above the ice" to "ascending *into the holiest by the blood of Jesus, By a new and living way, which he hath consecrated for us, through the veil* (third mention), *that is to say, his flesh.* These texts do not speak of a tearing of the veil. It is impossible, however, in reading them, not to think of it. It is a matter of crossing the second veil, of dispensing with corporeal appearances, the veil of the flesh, and entering the heavenly liturgy.

the holy mountain" or praying in the "upper chamber." Freemasonry evokes the "middle chamber."

Ascent of the holy mountain, risen to the upper chamber, or dwelling in the middle chamber: these are three images of the same experience. Let's explore them further.

The holy mountain

The mountain is the earth's closest place to heaven, which has always given it a sacred character. The mountain allows solitude. It recalls the ant-like scale of the human activity in the valley.

The mountain is prone to electrical condensations that are manifested by lightning and arouse the *tremendum* of the ancients. The mountain is often considered as the meeting point of heaven and earth: therefore a center, the point through which the axis of the world passes, which makes it a region saturated with the sacred.

The holy mountain

On Mount Zion, God made the Temple of Jerusalem for eternity.[43] Jesus dedicated his nights "to pray on the mountain." His essential message was the "Sermon on the Mount." Transfigured on Mount Tabor, he was crucified on Golgotha and "taken to heaven" on the Mount of Olives.

To reach the state required by the first quarantine, you must ascend to the holy mountain (Zion or Sinai). You must stick to it. *"Who shall ascend into the hill of Jehovah? And who shall stand in his holy place? He that hath clean hands, and a pure heart..."*[44] Stand in this place as long as possible: *"Lord, who may stay in your tent? Who may dwell on your holy mountain?"*[45]

---

43 Ps. 48.
44 Ps. 24:3-4.
45 Ps. 15:1-2.

The upper chamber

The scriptures state that meetings were usually held in the upper chamber. It was probably true in the literal sense. But this sense is not the only one. To assemble in the upper chamber is to work after having risen: *"There were many lights in the upper chamber, where they were gathered together."*[46]

The upper chamber

It is in this upper chamber that Elijah, the patron of Egyptian High Freemasonry, resurrects the son of the widow. Let us read the story again: *"After this the son of the woman, the mistress of the house, became ill. And his illness was so severe that there was no breath left in him... He [Elijah] said to her, 'Give me your son.' And he took him from her arms and carried him up into the upper chamber where he lodged... And the life of the child came into him again, and he revived. And Elijah took the child and brought him down from the upper chamber into the house and delivered him to his mother. And Elijah said, 'See, your son lives.'"*[47]

The middle chamber

A catechism of the Ancient and Accepted Scottish Rite teaches:
   Q. Where is the master mason?
   A. In the center of the circle.
   Q. Why in the center of the circle?
   A. Because this is the point from which he cannot err.
   The Masons of the Ancient and Primitive Rite of Memphis-Misraim are accustomed to write that they meet at the "Zenith of this or that city." By this, they recall that they meet in a place that is not a point of space, but an eternal meridian. Their meetings

---

46 Acts 20:8.
47 1 Kings 17:17-23.

are held in "the year 000 000 000 of the True Light." They can not be located on a timeline. They are beneath time.

The middle chamber

Even today, the chamber of the masters is called "the middle chamber." It is in the middle of the other two. Both the name and the layout are an image of this inner temple, of that center of the circle in which the Egyptian Mason cannot go astray. An ancient Italian text[48] calls it an *inner chamber (camera interiore)* and the catechism contained in *L'ordre des francs-maçons trahi*[49] calls it an *inner chamber* or a *middle chamber*. *Middle Chamber* is the name Prichard gives it in his *Masonry Dissected*.[50] In this room, says the catechism, the masters receive their salary. It is this, the least appropriate expression, that prevailed. There, the true mason can access the rest reserved for the solely-chosen masons of God, this *"peace which passeth all understanding"* evoked by Scripture.[51]

Cagliostro plays the architect

With genius, Cagliostro combines these three images and plays the architect. To proceed with our regeneration, he enjoins us to climb a mountain and to enter the pavilion at the top. Then, through a vertical hatch, we must climb into the upper chamber of this pavilion. The upper chamber is also a chamber in the middle... This upper chamber is blank and white in color, with no window open to the surrounding landscape. As in the Acts of the Apostles, we find a lamp suspended in the upper chamber where the operations take place.

---

48 *I Segreti dei Franchi Muratori* (Turin: 1762), p. 74.
49 Gabriel-Louis-Calabre Pérau, *L'ordre des francs-maçons trahi* (Amsterdam: 1745), p. 96.
50 Samuel Prichard, *Masonry Dissected* (London: J. Wilford, 1730).
51 Ph. 4:7.

Q. What sort of place is to be chosen for this important retreat?

A. One prefers a very high place, and if possible a mountain uninhabited and well hidden from the eyes of mortals, on which is built the pavilion according to the proper and convenient proportions; and one should tell no one of the day on which he will leave. It will be necessary to assemble in advance all the articles necessary, which are the instruments of the art according to Moses; the furniture; the utensils; the vestments; etc.

Q. What do you mean by the instruments of the art?

A. They are different objects, such as the ceremonial cloth and others. The ceremonial cloth is of yellow silk of which you will recognize the importance and the necessity, when you are instructed in the manner in which it will be necessary to consecrate the pavilion and the instruments of the art.

Q. What is the pavilion called?

A. Zion; to teach that it was on the Mount of Zion that God revealed himself to man.

Q. I beg of you to give me the details of the pavilion, including its dimensions.

A. The pavilion must be built expressly for that purpose and destroyed when that purpose has been fulfilled. It is three stories high. The chamber on the third floor should be a perfect square, eighteen feet in height as well as length and breadth. The four windows placed in the middle of each side should be oval, three feet high and four feet wide. There is but one door for entrance to this room, and it should be built in such a manner that each person alone may open or close it at will. This room should be entirely white, without any other color. The second chamber or cell in the middle story has no windows. It should be perfectly round and of a size to contain thirteen beds, solely for the repose of the twelve Elects and of the Chief. There should be a lamp in the middle; and there should only be such furniture as is absolutely necessary. When the third chamber is to be destroyed, the

How to Ascend to the Upper Chamber

second chamber will be called Ararat, to teach that the ark rested on the mountain and that perfect repose is destined for the Elect of God.
CAGLIOSTRO, *Catechism of the Egyptian Master*

Thus, the magician silences external sensory perceptions. He undertakes the ascent of the holy mountain to see the world as the Sun sees it. The only lamp he authorizes illuminates it from within himself. He climbs into the middle chamber to reach the center of the circle, in which he is no longer carried away by the movement of existence.

How to Ascend to the Middle Chamber

To operate effectively

If it were sufficient to know the "right" ritual and execute it perfectly to obtain results, a theatrical actor would reach the spiritual heights. That is not the key. To operate effectively, the Freemason must stand in the middle chamber.

You have experienced this state

How do you climb the mountain, then, in the pavilion situated at the summit? How do you get into the upper chamber? How can the master mason, concretely, access the middle chamber?

You have already climbed into the upper chamber. You have already touched this particular "state of grace." Suppose you have practiced a sport at a high level. You happened to have, during a competition, made the perfect gesture, the right gesture. Let's review some peculiarities of this phenomenon:

- this gesture has exceeded your usual expertise. By wanting it, you would not have managed to achieve it.
- to perform this gesture, you have not visualized anything. Thoughts, whether images or "positive" thoughts, have nothing to do with our practice.
- at the moment you became aware that you were in this state of grace, you said, "I am good today. I have to continue the

match with this momentum." Then, instantly, everything was ruined. You ended the game in great mediocrity.

This is true in any profession. From the blacksmith to the opera singer, every person who has mastered his art has experienced this state. Find the episodes of your life where you lived this experience. You will understand in which state your ritual must take place in order to be efficient.

A three-step process

How do you consciously access this particular state? Here are the three steps that will help you reproduce it.

I. Make the interior calm

Leave your metal at the door of the Temple. For this, access the inner calm. Shut the door to all your cogitation by sealing your own lodge.[52]

II. Enter the center of the circle

The master mason enters his laboratory in the middle chamber. He aligns with the vertical axis.

III. Stand in the center of the circle

In the center of the circle, a total silence reigns. The "I" no longer exists as a mark on a timeline or as a point in space. The mason master has the feeling that *it* thinks, that *it* unfolds. He is in the Holy of Holies, in the heart of the Temple, where, according to

---

52 Let the images pass by without stopping on one or the other. Don't try to think of nothing, that doesn't work! Work on the fear that touches you (fear of failure, fear of "dark forces," etc.), until you approach your ritual with benign neutrality. It is difficult, because you must find within yourself that point of serenity in which fear has no more hold on you. If you need five minutes, take them. If your work day has disturbed you and you need half an hour, take that too.

His promise, God speaks to Israel.

In this silent chamber, the activity of the Sublime Architect of All Worlds unfolds itself.[53] It gives birth to a new humanity. "God is a force," Dion Fortune wrote. Divinity is a river that never stops flowing. It is life being lived. It does not flow *through* you; it does not flow *by* you. No plumbing can imprison the divinity! In the center of the circle, *you* are the divinity flowing.

The consequences

Life is inevitable. Uniformity and rigidity will never stop it. By standing in the center of the circle, your being will regenerate and your existence will be restructured.

In the middle chamber, to quote Cagliostro, *"the man will no longer aspire to anything but perfect repose, in order to arrive at immortality, and he will be able to say of himself,* I AM THAT I AM.*"* Words which, according to the Bible, are those of God to Moses, from the burning bush.

---

53 As Hegel described in the *Encyclopedia of the Philosophical Sciences* (§ 379 A), the spirit is *"the real idea knowing itself,"* *"a necessary development of the eternal idea."*

When Philosophers Related This Experience

The Roman religion launched its last fires through a reaction of which Plotinus (205-270) was the most remarkable representative. Porphyry was his direct disciple. In this same "Neoplatonic" current, Iamblichus has left us the best advocacy ever written in favor of theurgy.

Plotinus describes the state that we seek to reproduce: *"Let us remember those moments when, here below, we are in a state of contemplation, in total clarity. At these moments, we make no regress onto ourselves, because of our intellectual activity: we alone are in possession of ourselves and our activity is entirely turned towards the object. We then become this object... we are no more than ourselves in power."*

(*Enneads* IV, 4, 2, 3)

To know how to look at the sensible world—the world perceptible to the senses—is to prolong the vision of the eye by a vision of the spirit. It is through a powerful effort of mental vision, piercing the material envelope of things and going to read the formula, invisible to the eye, that unfolds their materiality.

In ancient philosophy, "form" is a dynamic concept. The form is the "active mold," the "structuring matrix" that informs the material. It is the projection of the archetype in matter. The work is to go back to the world of forms, to go beyond the material appearances of things to see their form.

"Imagine the sensible world, with each of its parts remaining what it is, without any confusion, yet all together forming, as much as possible, a unity, so that if one of the parts manifests itself, the vision of others necessarily follows. For example suppose that the vision of the sphere of fixed stars is immediately followed by the vision of the sun and, at the same time, that of the other stars. Imagine that we see the earth, the sea, and all living things as in a transparent sphere, in which everything could appear. Let us have in the soul the luminous image of this sphere which contains everything in it. Keep this image in yourself and delete the mass; remove from it also the expense and the matter that are in your imagination."

PLOTINUS, Enneads (V 8, 9, 1); see also (II 9, 17, 4)

Unfortunately, only exceptional beings maintain themselves in this state. And every true master has experienced the experience described by Plotinus:

"Often I wake up to myself; I become external to other things and internal to myself; I see a beauty of wonderful majesty; so I believe it. I am, above all, from a superior world; the life I live then is the best life. I identify with the Divine, in him I have my home: having achieved this supreme activity, this is where I settle. I transcend all other spiritual reality; but, after this rest in the Divine, falling back from intuition in reflection and reasoning, I wonder then how I could ever, this time again, have come down thus, how my soul could never come to be inside a body, if already, while it is in this body, it is such as it appeared to me."

PLOTINUS, Enneads (IV 8, 1, 1)

www.ingramcontent.com/pod-product-compliance
Lightning Source LLC
Chambersburg PA
CBHW072013110526
44592CB00012B/1289